The Complete Learn Japanese for Adults Beginners Book (3 in 1)

Hiragana, Katakana, and Kanji
Master Reading, Writing, and Speaking Japanese with
This Simple 3 Step Process

Worldwide Nomad

Introduction

Welcome to the journey of learning Japanese!

You may be planning a trip to Japan, wanting to speak to a friend in Japanese, enjoy Japanese entertainment, or you may simply be attracted to its authentic culture. Whatever your motivation may be, Japanese is an incredible language to learn.

It is a challenging language to learn as it does not share similarities with western languages such as English. However, with the right resources, you will master the language effortlessly. With this guide/ grammar book, you will be guided through the basics of Japanese grammar in a manner that allows you to naturally absorb the language. You will also receive a list / lists of essential vocabulary in every lesson. Information in some chapters connect to others, allowing you to always refresh your memory, and learn the connections in the language.

The vocabulary presented in each lesson has been carefully selected. You may find some lessons contain more vocabulary than others. This simply depends on the intention of the lesson – some are dedicated more to grammar consolidation, while others are simply intended to build your vocabulary. Rest assured that by following the lessons, you will receive a balance of all aspects of the language.

With your dedication, you will not only master the basics of the language, but also have a deeper connection to Japanese culture. This guide has been designed for you to make rapid progress while enjoying your journey of discovering this new language. Enjoy the journey and best of luck!

Contents

JAPANESE PHRASEBOOK FOR BEGINNERS: LEARN COMMON PHRASES IN CONTEXT WITH EXPLANATIONS FOR EVERYDAY USE AND TRAVEL

JAPANESE SHORT STORIES FOR LANGUAGE LEARNERS: LEARN AND IMPROVE YOUR JAPANESE COMPREHENSION THROUGH 20 SHORT STORIES BASED OFF JAPAN'S CAPTIVATING HISTORY

FREE GIFT

Inside this gift you'll find:

Online Pronunciation Course: Easily perfect pronunciation through an online video course for audio learners

TO CLAIM BONUS:

Scan the QR Code below

OR

Visit the link below:

https://worldwidenomadbooks.com/Japanese-free-course

Japanese Hiragana, Katakana, and Kanji Workbook For Beginners:
Learn Japanese With Essential, Easy to Understand Lessons

Worldwide Nomad

CHAPTER 1:

Writing System and Pronunciation

1.1 kana world ~ hiragana and katakana~

The Japanese Language has 3 writing systems: Hiragana, Katakana and Kanji. Each of which is composed of different characters. The thought of having to master not one, not two, but *three* writing systems may seem overwhelming. However, it is not as difficult as you may think. In the English language, there are *many* ways of pronouncing and writing phonetics – i.e. one sound may be represented by different letters or a combination of letters. For example, the words "bel<u>ie</u>ve", "p<u>eo</u>ple", and "k<u>e</u>y". The underlined portion of the words are all the *same sound*, yet written in different ways. This is not something to worry about when learning Japanese. As long as we remember the combination of only **46 sounds**, we will have no problem reading or pronouncing.

Hiragana

The first writing system we will be introduced to is: Hiragana.

Hiragana can be said to be the foundation of the language, and thus this is where we will begin. Each character has only *one* syllable. The first row of the **Table of Hiragana Letters** (shown below), make up the 5 vowels – a, i, u, e, o. The characters in the following rows consist of the same vowels, the only difference being that they are preceded by a consonant. Let's take a look at the Table now:

Table of Hiragana Letters

あ / a	い / i	う / u	え / e	お / o
か / ka	き / ki	く / ku	け / ke	こ / ko
さ / sa	し / shi	す / su	せ / se	そ / so
た / ta	ち / chi	つ / tsu	て / te	と / to
な / na	に / ni	ぬ / nu	ね / ne	の / no
は / ha	ひ / hi	ふ / fu	へ / he	ほ / ho
ま / ma	み / mi	む / mu	め / me	も / mo
や / ya		ゆ / yu		よ / yo
ら / ra	り / ri	る / ru	れ / re	ろ / ro
わ / wa		を / wo		ん / n

→ Looking at the first row, you can see these characters represent the 5 vowels

→ As you move down the table, you can see each row consists of the *same vowels*, but simply has the addition of a consonant – i.e. the second row has the consonant 'k' before each vowel, the next has the consonant 's', and so on.

Katakana

The next writing system is: Katakana.

Katakana is also a syllabary. The characters represent the exact same sounds as Hiragana. You might be wondering, if they are the same sounds, what's the purpose of having Katakana? Katakana is mainly used to express words that are of a foreign origin. For example, the Japanese word for 'bread', is "pan" (パン). Since the word "pan" is of Spanish origin, we use Katakana to write the word!

Another important use of Katakana is for expressing onomatopoeic sounds. For example, when wanting to express a dog barking, you would say "wan wan" (ワンワン), which is meant to express the barking sound of a dog. We'll take a look at the Katakana characters alongside the Hiragana characters.

Table of Hiragana & Katakana Letters

あ・ア / a	い・イ / i	う・ウ / u	え・エ / e	お・オ / o
か・カ / ka	き・キ / ki	く・ク / ku	け・ケ / ke	こ・コ / ko
さ・サ / sa	し・シ / shi	す・ス / su	せ・セ / se	そ・ソ / so
た・タ / ta	ち・チ / chi	つ・ツ / tsu	て・テ / te	と・ト / to
な・ナ / na	に・ニ / ni	ぬ・ヌ / nu	ね・ネ / ne	の・ノ / no
は・ハ / ha	ひ・ヒ / hi	ふ・フ / fu	へ・ヘ / he	ほ・ホ / ho
ま・マ / ma	み・ミ / mi	む・ム / mu	め・メ / me	も・モ / mo
や・ヤ / ya		ゆ・ユ / yu		よ・ヨ / yo
ら・ラ / ra	り・リ / ri	る・ル / ru	れ・レ / re	ろ・ロ / ro
わ・ワ / wa		を・ヲ / wo		ん・ン / n

Do you notice something in the table of Hiragana and Katakana?

Some characters are so similar in shape, while others are completely different. Generally speaking, the Katakana scripts have *no* curvy strokes, which is something common in Hiragana, and Katakana scripts overall have less strokes. Some people say that having more strokes, like Hiragana, make them easier to memorize. What do you think?

It might be challenging to start memorizing all in a short period of time, but you can always refer to the Kana table every time you encounter new words. This will bring you closer to becoming a Kana expert one day!

Practice Japanese pronunciation with the aid of **Rōmaji**

✦ Quick explanation ✦

When looking at the Hiragana and Katakana tables, you will see that we use the letters of the alphabet. This is what is known as "Rōmaji", it is when we romanize the Japanese characters - i.e. use the Roman / Latin script - to aid in producing the respective sounds. Much more on this in a bit!

When practicing pronunciation, there are 2 sounds to be aware of.

1. "ra" (ら) - all the sounds in this column (this is the second last column on the Kana table).

Although in the Rōmaji system, the Japanese "ra" (ら) - column sounds are expressed with the romanized "r" letter, they are not the typical "r" sound that is produced with the rolling of the tongue. The actual sound is between the sound of a soft "r" to normal "l" sound.

Observe the placement of your tongue on the roof of your mouth as you are about to pronounce an "l" sound. You will realize that the tip of your tongue is very close to your front teeth. In order to pronounce the Japanese "ra" (ら) sound, move your tongue a little further back, and produce an "l" sound. This less intense "l" sound, which may sound a little similar to a soft "r" sound, is exactly what you are looking for!

2. "fu" (ふ) - the sound of just this one character.

Another point to pay attention to is the "fu" (ふ) sound. This is the only character in the column to be aware of. Although it is written with the letter "f", it is not the Western language pronunciation. "fu" (ふ) is a sound produced using more of your diaphragm, more like breathing sound of relief. It is interesting that it is not written as "hu", since the pronunciation is almost exactly "hu". Just keep in mind that the spelling may be with an "f", but you can remember it as a "hu" sound.

✦ How are you finding Rōmaji? Is the process of pronouncing all 46 letters easier with the guidance of Rōmaji? ✦

1.2 kanji

Let's move on to the explanation of Kanji now.

Kanji are Chinese characters that were adopted into the Japanese writing system. Unlike Hiragana and Katakana, which are just phonetic letters, Kanji are ideograms - they are characters that hold meaning. Among the thousands of Kanji characters, about 2,000 are commonly used in daily writing. Having learnt Hiragana and Katakana, you may be thinking that a *third* writing system is quite unnecessary, especially since Hiragana and Katakana already express *all* the Japanese phonetics. Just remember this thought you have, because you will find that thought changes as you advance with your grasp on the language. Although you will start to understand these points yourself in the later stages of your learning, for now, we'll look at two ways Kanji will prove to be *helpful* to your language learning journey:

1. Clarity

In the Japanese Language, we have a great number of homonyms, these are words that have the exact same pronunciation but completely different meanings. We see this in the word "Kanji" itself. "Kanji" can be written as "漢字", which refers to the writing system we are currently speaking of, but it can also can be written as "感じ", which means "feelings/emotions". If you were to be given *only* the Hiragana pronunciation, it would be difficult to decipher which word it is. You would have to really understand the context and then make a conclusion from there. However, with the Kanji characters, you will immediately know which word is being used.

2. Boundaries

Kanji dramatically improves the readability of the text not only by clarifying the homonyms, but also by allowing readers to know the boundaries of the words. In Japanese, *all* particles are written in Hiragana. Verbs and adjectives are written partially with Kanji, and *most* nouns are written in Kanji. Therefore, when reading a long sentence, you will be able to easily understand the sentence, as you will quite literally spot the boundaries by spotting the particles. Simply by recognising boundaries, you will see how quickly you can comprehend a passage or text!

Reading Kanji

Kanji is usually the last system to be learned, even for native Japanese.

One huge difference between Kanji from Kana (Hiragana and Katakana) is that there are multiple ways of pronouncing a single Kanji character. The reason for having multiple ways of reading is that there is an original Chinese way of reading it, which is called "on-yomi"(おんよみ), and a Japanese way of reading, which is called "kun-yomi" (くんよみ). When the Kanji writing system was incorporated into the Japanese Language, new pronunciations were added accordingly. So, if you start to see that one kanji has several pronunciations, you know why!

Learning Kanji is a lot of fun because they are hieroglyphics / pictographs, you can recognize some of the characters and you will know the meaning from its shape. In the long run they will prove to be very useful for reading comprehension at intermediate and advanced levels. One of the best things is that in the case that you do not know how to read a particular kanji, you are able to guess the meaning of the word simply by looking at the Kanji! However, we won't go into much of Kanji here, you will find much more about Kanji in Chapter 4, so more on that later.

1.3 Rōmaji

The Latin Alphabet can be used to write Japanese. It is called Rōmaji, which means "Roman Letters". Rōmaji is the romanization of the Japanese Language and it is very useful for Japanese Learners, especially for beginners, to spell out the pronunciation of characters.

For native Japanese, Rōmaji is used as the input for word processors and computers - you can also find it as an option (Japanese - Rōmaji) to add to the keyboard of your phone. You will also find Rōmaji on street signs or stations, for those who do not understand Kana and Kanji scripts.

Rōmaji is incredibly useful to bridge the gap between your native language and the Japanese language. However, if you are hoping to rely entirely on Rōmaji, it would not support you as you advance onto higher levels. There will be cases where Rōmaji cannot properly describe the pronunciations of characters / words. You will find that as we progress through this guide, you may even feel that the Kana and Kanji scripts are more beneficial. Nevertheless, all text in this guide is written using Rōmaji as it is designed for beginners who have no prior understanding of the Kana writing system.

1.4 Variation of Pronunciation on the Basic Sound

There are some variations of the basic sounds of Hiragana. Here, you will find 5 variations: Dakuon, Handakuon, Yōon, Sokuon, and Chōon.

1. DAKUON

"Dakuon" sounds are produced by placing the symbol ＿˙ on the upper right side of the Hiragana or Katakana character. This symbol can *only* be placed with Hiragana and Katakana from the second, third, fourth, and sixth rows. The table below summarizes *all* the Dakuon sounds:

DAKUON TABLE

が / ga	ぎ / gi	ぐ / gu	げ / ge	ご / go
ざ / za	じ / zi	ず / zu	ぜ / ze	ぞ / zo
だ / da	ぢ / zi	づ / zu	で / de	ど / do
ば / ba	び / bi	ぶ / bu	べ / be	ぼ / bo

Have you tried to pronounce all the "Dakuon" on the above table? You may have noticed that there are two sets of the same sounds, "じ" and "ぢ", along with "ず" and "づ". Although the pronunciation of these characters is the same when in Dakuon form, their original pronunciation are different - i.e. the original of "じ" (ji) is "し" (shi), and the original of "ぢ" (ji) is "ち" (chi). Therefore, although they have the same pronunciation, they are *not* interchangeable. Knowing when to use them simply depends on your knowledge of words, so don't get too stressed for now with when to use which character!

2. HANDAKUON

Now, instead of placing the ＿ symbol for Dakuon sounds, we place the ○ symbol on the upper right side of the Kana to produce "Handakuon" sounds. There is only *one* row in the Kana table that can produce Handakuon sounds, which is the sixth column.

These popping sounds are for these five letters only:

HANDAKUON TABLE

ぱ / pa	ぴ / pi	ぷ / pu	ぺ / pe	ぽ / po

3. YŌON

"Yōon" is described by i-column letters such as "き", "し", "ち", "に", "ひ", and "み" (ki, shi, chi, ni, hi, and mi) plus a **small** "や" (ya), "ゆ" (yu) or "よ" (yo) character. For example:

き (ki) + や (ya) = きゃ (kya).

It is important to note that the "や" (ya), "ゆ" (yu) or "よ" (yo) are written in a size **smaller** than the usual size. Although it may look subtle, there is a difference! Here are the "Yōon" sounds summarized in a table:

YŌON SOUNDS

きゃ / kya	きゅ / kyu	きょ / kyo
しゃ / sha	しゅ / shu	しょ / sho
ちゃ /cha	ちゅ /chu	ちょ / cho
にゃ /nya	にゅ /nyu	にょ / nyo
ひゃ /hya	ひゅ / hyu	ひょ / hyo
みゃ /mya	みゅ / myu	みょ / myo
りゃ / rya	りゅ / ryu	りょ / ryo

Some of these "Yōon" sounds can also be combined with "Dakuon". We would simply add the "Dakuon" symbol ＿ﾟ and produce the following:

YŌON + DAKUON SOUNDS

ぎゃ / gya	ぎゅ / gyu	ぎょ / gyo
じゃ / jya	じゅ / jyu	じょ / jyo
ぢゃ / jya	ぢゅ / jyu	ぢょ / jyo
びゃ /bya	びゅ / byu	びょ / byo

4. SOKUON

"Sokuon" is double consonant sound, and is the produced with **small** "つ" (tsu). It is very similar to the above concept of "Yōon", but this time the character that is being used is "つ" (tsu). It is used to mark a geminate consonant, which is formed by doubling the following consonant. Once again, it is written in **half the size or smaller** of the original "つ" (tsu) as seen in the examples. Distinguishing the double consonant is important, as they can also change the meaning of a word. Here are a few examples of how the single and double consonant words are of different meanings:

きて (kite) = to come

vs

きって (ki<u>tte</u>) = a stamp used for mailing

—

さか (saka) = slope

vs

さっか (sa<u>kk</u>a) = author, novelist, writer

If you find this "Sokuon" explanation too complicated, just remember that when you see the **small** つ (tsu), that is the sign of a "Sokuon". Pronouncing this just requires a slight pause after the first Hiragana, and moving into the second Hiragana. Now that you have seen both "Yōon" and "Sokuon", you can rest assured that those are the *only* Hiragana that can be **small**, no other hiragana apart from や (ya), ゆ (yu), よ(yo), and つ (tsu) can be small.

5. CHŌON

In contrast to "Sokuon" where you have a slight pause between Hiragana, there is also this variation whereby the pronunciation of words is extended. This variation is called, "Chōon". We simply add an extra corresponding vowel "a" (あ), "i" (い), or "u" (う), to the vowel where the elongation is necessary. It may be easier to understand if we break it down into each of the rules:

1. For vowels ending with "a" (あ), add on an extra "a" (あ) sound.

おかあさん (okāsan) = mother

The third character, "a" (あ), is the added sound to extend the pronunciation. This is because the character before that is "ka" (か), and it ends with an "a" sound. You can also see where the added sound is placed by looking at the Rōmaji. The line right above the 'a' letter in 'okāsan' is written with a short line 'ā', signifying this word is in fact a variation.

2. Vowels ending with "e" (え) are followed by an extra "e" (え) or "i" (い).

えいが (eiga) = movie

—

おねえさん (oneesan) = older sister

Although the Rōmaji may not have a distinct spelling, you can understand that there is the extra vowel by looking at the spelling. For example, "eiga" has the "i", and "oneesan" has an extra "e" as well.

3. Vowels ending with the sound of "o" (お), are extended with an "u" (う) sound.

おはよう (ohayō) = good morning

* There is an exception to this rule! In some cases, we would extend it with another (o) sound. For example,

おおきい (ōkii) = big

We have seen how to use "Chōon" with Hiragana characters, but in this case, it does not work the same way with Katakana characters. Instead of adding a corresponding vowel sound, the long vowel is simply represented by a dash "ー". For example:

コーヒー (kōhī) = coffee

—

スーパーマーケット (sūpāmāketto) = supermarket

These are both words that are written in Katakana form, since they are of foreign origin. We can see that the Rōmaji of these words are useful in indicating where the vowel is to be extended, and where we place the dash.

The importance of including the long vowel is important, because a wrong pronunciation will change the meaning of a word entirely. We'll look at some of these examples now:

おばさん (obasan) = aunt

vs

おばあさん (obāsan) = grandmother

—

おじさん (ojisan) = uncle

vs

おじいさん (ojīsan) = grandfather

—

ビル (biru) = building

vs

ビール (bīru) = beer

—

かど (kado) = corner

vs

カード (kādo) = card

✦ Quick Review ✦

We have covered a lot so far, so let's do a quick revision of everything we have seen!

Hiragana	あ・い・う・え・お
Katakana	ア・イ・ウ・エ・オ
Rōmaji	A・I・U・E・O
Dakuon	Add the ＿ ﹅ symbol at the upper right-hand corner of the character
Handakuon	Add the ○ symbol at the upper right-hand corner of the character
Yōon	Add a **small** や・ゆ・よ
Sokuon	Add a **small** つ / Double consonant sound
Chōon	Adding an extra vowel / Long vowel sounds

Now that we have this table to guide us, we are going to take everything we have learnt and put it into practice! We will do some reading, a little bit of writing, and then you will have completed your first chapter!

Exercise 1.1

Practice reading the following Japanese words in Rōmaji while looking at the Hiragana script. Where there is the (   ) space, fill it in with the appropriate hiragana.

Rōmaji	Hiragana	Meaning
Kodomo	(　)ども	child / children
Kazoku	かぞく	family
Ie	(　)え	house
Uchi	うち	house /home
Gakkou	が (　)こう	school
Mise	み(　)	shop
Eki	えき	station
Tomodachi	と(　)だち	friend
Sensei	せんせい	teacher
Nihon go	にほん(　)	Japanese language
Benkyō	べんき(　)う	study (noun)
Hon	ほん	a book

Ki	き	tree
Sanpo	さん（　）	stroll
Hito	ひと	person

Exercise 1.2

For each of the countries 1-8, match it to its corresponding city mentioned from a-h.

(Feel free to use your Katakana table to read the names of countries and cities.)

1) イタリア	a. カイロ
2) ブラジル	b. ニューデリー
3) エジプト	c. ホーチミン
4) インド	d. リスボン
5) ベトナム	e. パリ
6) ポルトガル	f. モスクワ
7) フランス	g. ローマ
8) ロシア	h. リオデジャネイロ

☑Check list #1

Do you know how to say words in Japanese?

☐ Tree

☐ Family

☐ Station

☐ Book

☐ Study

☐ Japanese language

☐ Friend

☐ Shop

Nihongo Trivia

~Right to Left? Left to Right?~

Modern Japanese can be written from left to right in horizontal lines, as we normally observe in English. This way of Japanese writing is called "YOKOGAKI" (よこがき / 横書き) - the word "yoko" (よこ / 横) means "side" or "besides", so "Yokogaki" refers to "horizontal writing". However, traditionally, Japanese has been written in vertical columns. The scripts were read from top to bottom and from right to left. This way of writing is called "TATEGAKI" (たてがき / 縦書き) - the word "tate" (たて / 縦) means "straight up" or "longitudinal", and thus "Tategaki" means "vertical writing".

In this book, everything is written in "YOKOGAKI" to be easy for Japanese learners. You will also observe the Kana Charts have been written in "YOKOGAKI" style; however, Japanese native children learn Hiragana with "TAKEGAKI" charts. If you search for a Hiragana chart online, you may find it in either "YOKOGAKI" or "TATEGAKI" styles. This is the same for any exercise books that you purchase. Just keep this in mind so that there will be no confusion for you!

CHAPTER 2:

Noun sentences: Simply Introducing Yourself!

Unlike the western languages, the nouns in Japanese have neither a declension, nor a formal distinction of number (singular or plural), nor an article (definite or indefinite). No gender, no number, and no articles to pay attention to! What a relief! It is quite straightforward when it comes to forming noun sentences – it is simply a matter of memorizing the basic patterns.

You may be feeling slightly suspicious to hear that it is actually easy to string words together to form sentences. In some cases, the word order is flexible as well! It's probably hard to believe right now, so let's just get straight into sentence structures.

2.1 – wa – desu (positive sentences)

Let's take a look at the following sentence patterns with nouns.

Noun A wa Noun B desu

Noun A は Noun B です

Meaning: Noun A is Noun B

*Please take note that "は" should be read as "wa" when it is used as a topic marker particle, the same sound as "わ".

The particle "wa" (は)indicates that the Noun A is the topic of the sentence, we call it a "topic marker". Once we are presented with the topic marker by adding "wa" (は) after the noun, then we can add information to create a statement about the topic.

WATASHI WA ANNA DESU.

わたし は アンナ です。

Meaning: I am Anna.

Adding "desu" (です) after (noun B) at the end of the sentence forms a predicate.

2.2 — wa — dewa arimasen (negative sentences)

Now let's look at the sentence patterns of negative sentences.

<u>Noun A</u> wa <u>Noun B</u> dewa arimasen

<u>Noun A</u> は <u>Noun B</u> では ありません

Meaning: Noun A is not Noun B

* The "は" from "dewa arimasen" in this sentence structure is also read as "wa".

<u>WATASHI</u> WA <u>ARISU</u> DEWA ARIMASEN.

<u>わたし</u> は <u>アリス</u> では ありません。

Meaning: <u>I</u> am not <u>Alice.</u>

Let's try to form some sentences using the vocabularies listed below.

Rōmaji	Hiragana	Meaning
watashi	(わたし/ 私)	I
anata	(あなた)	you
gakusei	(がくせい/ 学生)	student

kaishain	(かいしゃいん/ 会社員)	company employee
*~san	(さん)	suffix to someone's name
*~jin	(じん/ 人)	stating Nationality

* "～san" is often placed after someone's name to show respect to that person. It is rare to call someone without this suffix. It is only unless you have established a very close relationship to a person that you would not use it, or of course, if you are speaking with friends that are of the same age as you.

* "～jin" is used to describe someone's nationality. Stating the name of the country followed by "jin", is the word for the nationality of that country. For example,

アメリカ (country)   +   じん / 人   =   アメリカじん (American)

フランス (country)   + じん / 人   =   フランスじん/人 (French)

It will be useful to know countries and nationalities, so the table below includes many countries. Notice how they are written in Katakana since they are foreign words!

Rōmaji	Katakana	English
amerika	アメリカ	America
igirisu	イギリス	England
kanada	カナダ	Canada
furansu	フランス	France
doitsu	ドイツ	Germany
betonamu	ベトナム	Vietnam
tai	タイ	Thailand
indo	インド	India
burajiru	ブラジル	Brazil
shingapōru	シンガポール	Singapore
ōsutoraria	オーストラリア	Australia
finrando	フィンランド	Finland
toruko	トルコ	Turkey

If you didn't find your country there, maybe it is one that is *not* expressed in Katakana! There are a few countries that are expressed in Kanji instead of Katakana, let's see them:

Rōmaji	Kanji	English
chūgoku	中国	China
kankoku	韓国	Korea
nihon	日本	Japan

Now that you have quite a few words to work with, feel free to start playing around with them! Create some positive sentences "— wa — desu" (— は — です)and negative sentences " — wa — dewa arimasen"(— は — ではありません) . Here are some you can look at to start off with:

WATASHI WA GAKUSEI DESU.

わたし は がくせい です。

Meaning: I am a student

—

WATASHI WA KAISHAIN DEWA ARIMASEN.

わたし は かいしゃいん では ありません。

Meaning: I am *not* a company employee

—

ANNA SAN WA AMERIKA JIN DESU.

アンナ さん は アメリカ じん です。

Meaning: Anna is an American.

—

ANNA SAN WA FURANSU JIN DEWA ARIMASEN.

アンナ さん は フランス じん では ありません。

Meaning: Anna is not French.

—

2.3 Noun sentences with Particle "MO"

Previously we learned that the particle "wa" (は) indicates the topic of the sentence, and we call it a topic marker. In this section, we will have a look at another topic marker, "mo" (も). You do not need to worry about having so many topic markers and getting confused. The particle "mo" (も) is used in place of "wa" (は) when the statement about the topic is the same as the topic in a previous sentence. It may be much easier to look at the examples.

ANNA SAN WA GAKUSEI DESU.

アンナさん は がくせい です。

Meaning: Anna is a student.

—

ARISU SAN MO GAKUSEI DESU.

アリスさん も がくせい です。

Meaning: Alice is also a student.

—

Now that we have looked at the example sentences, you must have understood what the particle "mo" (も) is. Yes! It is used to express "too", "also "or "as well." It is always related to the precedent noun.

There is another meaning of "mo" (も) when it is not used as a topic marker. But we will first work with "mo" (も) as a topic marker.

"ME, TOO" in Japanese conversation

In *any* conversation that you interact with, it is always nice to feel a connection or relation to the person you are speaking to, isn't it? In such experiences, you would most likely want to express how much you relate to the other person. With that being said, learning how to say "me too" in Japanese would be essential, wouldn't it?

The good news is that by now, you already know how to say it! In this chapter, we have learned the word, "watashi" (わたし). Now, we have learned the word, "mo" (も). And what happens when we just put these two together? We create:

WATASHI MO!

わたしも!

Meaning: "Me too!"

And although it is completely fine to use "watashi mo" (わたしも) to express "me too", there are actually a few variations to it. This is because there are a number of ways to say "me" in Japanese.

The word "watashi" (わたし) is both a polite and gender neutral word which can mean "I" or "me", depending on the context. This word is mostly used by non-natives who speak Japanese, as well as Japanese females. Men use this only in formal situations, because there are other options men have to refer to themselves when in more casual situations.

The word "boku" (ぼく) is used predominantly by men, in more relaxed situations. The word "ore" (おれ) is also used by men as well, but it has a more rough or tough feeling than the previous word "boku" (ぼく).

With that being said, let's summarize *all* the ways to express "me too" in Japanese:

わたしも

WATASHI MO

—

ぼくも

BOKU MO

(male)

—

おれも

ORE MO

(male)

—

2.4 Questions in Noun sentences

Having learned the sentence structures, creating a question is very simple. There is only one step to take in order to change the sentence into its question form.

You can change the noun sentence into a question form by simply adding "ka" (か) at the end of the sentence.

Question Form:

Noun A wa Noun B desu + ka

Noun A は Noun B です + か

There is absolutely no need to change the order of the words as is done in English. This rule of adding "ka" (か) at the end of a sentence can be applied to verb sentences as well as adjective sentences, which are sentence types that we are going to learn in a later chapter.

Let's look at examples using the sentences that you have already familiarize yourself with from the previous sections.

ANNA SAN WA GAKUSEI DESU KA.

アンナ さん は がくせい です か。

Meaning: Is Anna a student?

—

ANNA SAN WA AMERIKA JIN DESU KA.

アンナ さん は アメリカ じん です か。

Meaning: Is Anna an American?

—

Now that we know how to ask a question in Japanese, the next step would be to know how to *reply* to questions in Japanese. Let's start off with Yes / No questions. When we wish to reply, "Yes", we would say, "hai" (はい). When we wish to reply with a "No", we would answer, "iie" (いいえ). Let's see this in practice!

Question:

ANNA SAN WA GAKUSEI DESU KA.

アンナ さん は がくせい です か。

Meaning: <u>Is Anna a student</u>?

The possible answers would be:

HAI, GAKUSEI DESU.

はい、 がくせい です。

Meaning: Yes, she is a student.

//

IIE, GAKUSEI DEWA ARIMASEN.

いいえ、 がくせい では ありません。

Meaning: No, she is not a student.

—

✦ Quick Review ✦

These basic noun sentences of <u>Noun A</u> は <u>Noun B</u> です / <u>Noun A</u> is <u>Noun B</u> provides some information on Noun A, the topic. It is useful for introducing yourself, such as your name, nationality, profession, etc.

By adding "ka" (か) at the end of the sentence to make it "desuka" (ですか), you will have created a sentence and are able to initiate a conversation.

✦ Grammar Review ✦

☆ "wa" (は) is the particle indicating a topic, the topic marker.

☆ "mo" (も) is also a topic marker meaning "also".

☆ Adding "desu" (です) after (noun B) forms a predicate.

☆ Instead of "desu" (です), adding "dewa arimasen" (ではありません) or "ja arimasen" (じゃありません) forms negative sentences.

☑Check list #2

Can you answer the following questions?

☐ Sentences with topic marker "wa", will end with?

☐ Topic marker which has a meaning of "also".

☐ In negative sentence, "desu" changes to?

☐ What does "ja arimasen" mean?

☐ How to say "yes" and "no" in japanese?

☐ What does a Japanese full stop look like?

2.5 Punctuation

Japanese comma and full stop.

The Japanese punctuation you encountered when you first began studying the language might have surprised you since it is quite different from those in other languages.

Japanese Comma

The Japanese comma is called "tōten" (とうてん) and its role is to separate elements within the sentences. It is written as " 、 " and the usage is incredibly liberal compared to English. It is best to start observing its use in the context of books, newspapers, and magazines, since there is no exact definition of where it should be put. The main function is, of course, to give a reader an adequate pause in reading.

Japanese Full Stop

You may have already noticed in the example sentences presented so far.

The Japanese full stop is a little circle "。", called "kuten" (くてん).

There is a casual name for it as well, and it is called "maru" (まる), which simply means "circle". In formal Japanese writing, we do not use question marks when sentences are in the question form. Instead, we use a full stop, or "maru" (まる), even when a question is being written.

2.6 Phrases of Greetings

Greetings are important in many cultures and languages. There are many greeting phrases in Japanese, each with their own unique usage. It is essential to master how to greet as a first step in learning language.

Let's look at the most common and basic greetings in Japanese.

1. Ohayō gozaimasu (おはようございます)

"Ohayō gozaimasu" is equivalent to "Good Morning" in English and is typically used in the morning hours before noon as a greeting. The word for "morning" is not included in this phrase, but the part of "ohayō" comes from the word, "hayai" which means "early".

When you are greeting your close friends or family member, you can just say "ohayō", without "gozaimasu" as the part of " gozaimasu" makes the phrase more polite.

2. Konnichiwa (こんにちは)

"Konnichiwa" can be roughly translated as "hello" and is commonly used during the daytime between around noon to 5 or 6pm. The literal translation of "Konnichiwa" is "today is", and it came from the phrase like "how are you today?" and eventually shortened to left with only the topic part. Therefore "wa" from "konnichiwa" is a topic marker and written as "は".

3. Konbanwa (こんばんは)

You can use "Konbanwa" after sunset, probably after around 6pm, which roughly can be translated as "Good Evening". Again the literal translation of "konban" is "this evening" or "tonight", and it came from the phrase like " how are you this evening?". The "は" is read as "wa" – this is the same for "konnichiwa".

4. Oyasuminasai (おやすみなさい)

This is translated as "good night" and the literal translation is something very close to " Have a good rest". This phrase originated from the verb "yasumu" "yasumimasu" which means " to take a rest' or "be absent from". The shorter version of "Oyasumi" can be used among close friends or family members.

5. Arigatō gozaimasu (ありがとうございます)

It is a phrase to express your appreciation, translated as "Thank you". If you are in a casual situation, you can say "arigatō" whereas in a more formal situation, you would place the word "dōmo" before, and use the phrase "dōmo arigatō gozaimasu". It is one of the most important phrases to remember as a language learner beginner.

6. Ittekimasu / Itterasshai (いってきます / いってらっしゃい)

These phrases are unique in Japanese culture, which are commonly used between family members in a household. The person leaving the house greets "ittekimasu" which means "I am leaving and I'll be back" , and the person who is sending the family member off replies "itterasshai".

7. Tadaima / Okaerinasai (ただいま / おかえりなさい)

This is another set of phrases that are unique in Japanese, a set of greetings when someone comes back home. "Tadaima" can be translated to " I'm back home" and "Okaerinasai" can be translated to "welcome back home."

8. "Hajimemashite" (はじめまして)

This greeting word, "Hajimemashite" (はじめまして) is originated from the word "Hajimete"(はじめて) which means "for the first time". Therefore "Hajimemashite" is an acknowledgement of meeting someone for the first time. The translation would be "nice to meet you (for the first time.)"

It is used at the beginning of your introduction and it's one of the first phrases you can use when you meet someone new. It is a simple and polite phrase that is suitable to use when meeting anyone, regardless of age or status.

☑Check list #3

Can you say these greeting phrases in Japanese?

☐ "Nice to meet you"

☐ "Thank you"

☐ "Good moring"

☐ "Hello"

☐ "Good night"

☐ "Good evening"

Exercise 2

Rearrange the words to form the sentences that correspond to the English sentence in the bracket.

1. sensei / maiku-san wa / ka / desu (Is Mike a teacher?)

2. gakusei / watashi / wa / dewa arimasen (I am not a student.)

3. mo / anna-san / gakusei / desu (Anna is also a student.)

4. nihonjin / dewa / arimasen (I am not Japanese.)

Nihongo Trivia

~Don't Use "ANATA"?!~

The impression made by the word "you" in Japanese is different from in English.

We listed on the vocab table in this chapter the word "ANATA" which means "you". But generally this word doesn't appear in our conversation. "ANATA" is only used when there is no other way to address the person or know the person's name. In most cases you can address the person with their name plus suffix. Directly addressing people by using the word "ANATA" is actually considered a somewhat rude act.

You may wonder if you want to know someone's name and need to ask "what is YOUR name?" Well, even in this case, we are not using the word "your". Instead we make the noun "name" to its polite form so that the listener will know that the speaker is asking his/ her name.

"Name" in Japanese is "namae" (なまえ), and we can place "o" (お) in front of the noun "namae" and simply ask someone's name by saying "onamae wa? (おなまえは？) The more details are explained in the chapter 6 /6.2 honorific.

CHAPTER 3:

The Adjective sentences

Adjectives are not only essential for forming sentences but also making our sentences more interesting and colorful ones. With adjectives, we are able to express different emotions, and provide more detailed descriptions of people, places and things. Adjectives give us the power to add depth to our sentences. They are also very useful when we make comparisons between two or more things. The use of adjectives can make our written language as well as our spoken language / conversations more engaging and enjoyable. So, are we ready to take on some Japanese adjectives?

3.1 Two types of Adjectives

In Japanese all adjectives fall into two categories: i-adjectives and na-adjectives.

The adjectives whose basic form ends with the syllable "i" (い)are called i-adjectives. Obviously those adjectives ending with the syllable "na" (な) are called na-adjectives.

The reason we need to categorize the adjectives into two is because they each have their own conjugation – i.e. they form sentences in different ways.

Before we start making sentences, we will practice making simple phrases as you get to know a few examples of adjectives.

i-adjective

Let's start by looking at some examples of i-adjectives. If you have some experience with Japanese anime, you may already know some i-adjectives such as " oishii" (おいしい) or "kawaii"(かわいい) as they are well known Japanese words. And here you already have two examples of i-adjectives!

More examples of some useful i-adjectives:

Rōmaji	Hiragana / Kanji	Meaning
ATARASHII	あたらしい / 新しい	new
OMOSHIROI	おもしろい / 面白い	interesting
TANOSHII	たのしい / 楽しい	enjoyable

The adjectives' function is to modify nouns – to describe and to provide more details about nouns. Adjectives can be placed right before the noun that is to be modified.

For instance, if you are describing a book (noun) as new (adjective):

ATARASHII + HON (book) = ATARASHII HON

あたらしい　ほん

Meaning: A new book.

We can continue describing a book (noun) with the i-adjectives mentioned in the table above, to create the following phrase:

OMOSHIROI HON

おもしろい　ほん

Meaning: Interesting book

//

TANOSHII HON

たのしい　ほん

Meaning: Enjoyable / Fun book

—

na-adjective

Now we'll look at some examples of useful na-adjectives.

Rōmaji	Hiragana / Kanji	Meaning
SUKINA	すきな / 好きな	be fond of / like

KIREINA	きれいな	beautiful / clean
YŪMEINA	ゆうめいな / 有名な	famous

We will continue using "book" as our noun, and now we will use these na-adjectives to create some phrases to describe this "book".

SUKI NA HON

すき な ほん

Meaning: The book that someone is fond of

—

KIREI NA HON

きれい な ほん

Meaning: Beautiful book / Clean book

—

YŪMEI NA HON

ゆうめい な ほん

Meaning: Famous book

—

We have been using this rule to create the above phrases:

> i- adjective　〜い　+　Noun
>
> na-adjective　〜な　+　Noun
>
> Meaning: Both describe something about the noun

Simply combining the i-adjective or the na-adjective with a noun that you are speaking of. Now, as we move on to creating sentences with the i- and na-adjectives, we need to follow a different set of rules.

* Note: When wanting to create sentences such as "this is an interesting book", we would need to know about demonstrative nouns such as "this" and "that". These words will be covered in Chapter 5 / KOSOADO words.

We can form adjective sentences using the sentence pattern (— wa — desu) that we have already learned in the previous chapter.

Noun   wa   i-adjective   desu
⌣   は   〜〜〜い   です。

Noun   wa   na-adjective dsu
⌣   は   〜〜〜な   です。

Caution: the na-adjective "na" will be dropped

Now using this formula, let's describe "Anna san" (noun), with both i-adjectives and na-adjectives.

ANNA SAN WA OMOSHIROI DESU.

アンナ さん は　おもしろい　です。

Meaning: Anna is an interesting person.

—

ANNA SAN WA KIREI DESU.

アンナ さん は　きれい です。

Meaning: Anna is beautiful.

—

Don't worry if you're feeling a bit confused with this sentence structure, because it is a little tricky. When we use a na-adjective, in this case, "kireina" (きれいな), the "na" (な) has to be dropped when it joins with "desu" (です). When the "na" (な) is removed, it looks like it could be an i-adjective. This is why knowing which category the adjective falls into is important – so there will be no further confusion when it comes to forming grammatically correct sentences! However, knowing the category of the adjective is also all about time and practice, once your practice is consistent, you'll realize how easily you just *know* which adjective belongs to which category.

Good News!

The reason why the above example of the na-adjective was a bit tricky was because the sound *before* the "na" (な) is an "i" (い) sound. The good news is that na-adjectives which have this "i" (い) sound before "na" (な) are limited in number! These are written out in the table below, and so we just need to pay attention to these tricky ones:

Rōmaji	Hiragana / Kanji	Meaning
SUKINA	すきな / 好きな	be fond of / like
KIREINA	きれいな	beautiful / clean
YŪMEINA	ゆうめいな / 有名な	famous
BENRINA	べんりな / 便利な	convenient
GENKINA	げんきな / 元気な	healthy and energetic

Apart from the tricky ones, here is a list of common and useful na-adjectives:

Rōmaji	Hiragana / Kanji	meaning
SHIZUKANA	しずかな /静かな	quiet
NIGIYAKANA	にぎやかな	crowded and lively

SHINSETSUNA	しんせつな / 親切な	kind hearted
HIMANA	ひまな / 暇な	free (concerning time)
KANTANNA	かんたんな / 簡単な	easy and simple

ANNA SAN WA SHINSETSU DESU

アンナ さん は しんせつ です。

Meaning: Anna is kind.

ANNA SAN WA SHINSETU NA GAKUSEI DESU.

アンナ さんは しんせつ な がくせい です。

Meaning: Anna is a kind student.

—

Hopefully by now you are very clear about the difference in making sentences with na-adjectives. Are you getting confident in making adjective sentences?

3.2 vocab list

The adjectives listed above were just a few, and most definitely not a well-rounded list. Here is a section dedicated *solely* to building your vocabulary of adjectives.

Adjectives for Size and Weight

Big / ŌKII (おおきい)　　　　　　　　　Small / CHIISAI (ちいさい)

Tall / TAKAI (たかい)　　　　　　　　　Short in height / HIKUI (ひくい)

long/ NAGAI (ながい)　　　↔　　　　Short / MIJIKAI (みじかい)

Wide/ HIROI (ひろい)　　　　　　　　　Narrow / SEMAI (せまい)

Thick /FUTOI (ふとい)　　　　　　　　　Thin / HOSOI (ほそい)

Heavy /OMOI (おもい)　　　　　　　　　Light in weight / KARUI (かるい)

Adjectives for Characteristics

Delicious / OISHII (おいしい)   Disgusting / MAZUI (まずい)

Beautiful / KIREINA (きれいな)   Ugly / MINIKUI (みにくい)

Expensive / TAKAI (たかい)   Cheap / YASUI (やすい)

Hot / ATSUI (あつい)   Cold / SAMUI (さむい)

Old / FURUI (ふるい)   New / ATARASHII (あたらしい)

Bright / AKARUI (あかるい)   ↔   Dark / KURAI (くらい)

Clean / SEIKETSUNA (せいけつな)   Dirty / KITANAI (きたない)

Soft / YAWARAKAI (やわらかい)   Hard / KATAI (かたい)

Strong / TSUYOI (つよい)   Weak / YOWAI (よわい)

Safe / ANZENNA (あんぜんな)   Dangerous / KIKENNA (きけんな)

Deep / FUKAI (ふかい)   Shallow / ASAI (あさい)

Fast / HAYAI (はやい)   Slow / OSOI (おそい)

Busy / ISOGASHII (いそがしい)   Free / HIMANA (ひまな)

Difficult / MUZUKASHII (むずかしい)   Easy/ KANTANNA (かんたんな)   Quiet   /

SHIZUKANA (しずかな)   *Noisy /URUSAI (うるさい) or

*Lively/ NIGIYAKANA (にぎやかな)

*Both "URUSAI" and "NIGIYAKANA"can be the opposite of "SHIZUKANA". While "urusai" has a negative nuisance in it, "nigiyakana" has a more positive meaning.

You may have observed that in a lot of these pairs, it looks like they have a pattern of i-adjective pairing with an i-adjective, or na-adjective pairing with a na-adjective. However, this is *not* the case.

The opposite words can either be an i-adjective or a na-adjective, so unfortunately we don't have any shortcuts here…

3.3 negative form of adjective sentences

So far we have looked at creating positive sentences with i- and na-adjectives. Now, let's look at creating negative sentences.

i-adjective

い です ⇨ くないです

na-adjective

な です ⇨ なではありません

To change an i-adjective to its negative form, we need to remove the "i" (い) at the end of the adjective and replace it with "kunai" (くない) + "desu" (です).

To change a na-adjective to its negative form, we need to remove the "na" (な), and end the sentence with "dewa arimasen" (ではありません) instead of "desu" (です). And if you remember, this is the same way we learned negative noun sentences in the previous chapter! If it doesn't ring a bell, no worries, you *will* get the hang of things!

One exception of i-adjectives

There is one i-adjective that you need to take note of when turning it to its negative form. That adjective is "ii" (いい), which means "good". For this adjective, the negative form is "yokunai"(よくない). It may seem a bit tricky, but if you are familiar with the other way to say "good", then it may be easier to remember. Although "good" is "ii" (いい), and is the common and casual way to describe "good", you can also refer to something being good as "yoi" (よい). From this, you can apply to rule of removing the "i" (い) and adding "kunai" (くない) to create the negative form, "yokunai" (よくない).

Example Usage & Exercises

Using only the vocabularies you have been shown, let's try to make adjective sentences in their negative forms.

Let's say when you would like to convey the message: "I am not busy".

The adjective for busy is, "isogashii" (いそがしい). So this is the adjective that we will need to change to a negative form. We can use "watashi" (わたし) to refer to 'I', and create:

いそがし~~い~~ ⇨ いそがしくない + です

⇩

WATASHI WA ISOGASHIKUNAI DESU.

わたし は いそがしくない です。

Meaning: I am not busy

—

How about if you would like to say: " I am not free."

The adjective for "free" is "himana" (ひまな), a na-adjective. This means we have to use the na-adjective rule to create its negative form.

ひまな ⇨ ひま + ではありません

⇩

WATASHI WA HIMA DEWA ARIMASEN.

わたし は ひま ではありません。

Meaning: I am not free

—

3.4 Questions in adjective sentences

Again, as with noun sentences, making question sentences of adjective sentences is very simple. By simply adding "ka" (か) at the end of the sentence, adjective sentences change into their question form.

Some simple examples are shown below:

ANNA SAN WA SHINSETSU DESU KA.

アンナ さん は しんせつ ですか。

Meaning: Is Anna kind?

—

ANNA SAN WA OMOSHIROI DESUKA.

アンナ さん は おもしろい ですか。

Meaning: Is Anna an interesting person?

—

Example Usage

So far we seem to be making sentences about Anna-san or about "I". Let's try to make questions with a different topic. The sentence structure does *not* change at all, but this is just to provide a different way of creating a sentence.

Tokyo will be the Noun A – the topic, so we can start the sentences with "とうきょう は" (Tokyo wa...)

TOKYO WA NIGIYAKA DESUKA?

とうきょう は にぎやか ですか。

Meaning: Is Tokyo crowded / lively?

—

TOKYO WA ANZEN DESUKA?

とうきょう は あんぜん ですか。

Meaning: Is Tokyo safe?

—

Providing answers for these questions is the exact same formula as for noun sentences.

HAI NIGIYAKA DESU.

はい、 にぎやか です。

Meaning: Yes, it is crowded / lively.

//

IIE ANZEN DEWA ARIMASEN.

いいえ、 あんぜん では ありません。

Meaning: No, it is not safe.

—

Hopefully everything is clear with adjective sentences, including negative forms and question forms. All you have to do is to pay attention to the categories of the adjective (na-adjective or i-adjective) and follow the rules accordingly!

☑Check list #4

Can you form these adjective sentences in Japanese?

☐ "The shop is big / wide."

☐ "Is the teacher kind?"

☐ "Is the child healthy / energetic?"

☐ "Is Japanese difficult?"

☐ "Japanese is fun."

☐ "Sushi is not yummy."

Exercise 3

Create the negative form of each of the following. Don't forget to identify whether it is an i-adjective or a na-adjective, so that you can change it correctly!

1. いそがしい です (isogashii desu) ⇨

2. きれい です (kirei desu) ⇨

3. あつい です (atsui desu) ⇨

4. ひま です (hima desu) ⇨

5. いい です (ii desu) ⇨

Nihongo Trivia

~KAWAII CULTURE~

One of the more well-known Japanese words is "かわいい" (kawaii), as the Japanese pop culture or what is called the "KAWAII CULTURE" is getting very popular. It is spreading and gaining its popularity outside of Japan as well. "かわいい" (kawaii) means "cute", "adorable", or "lovable". The word contains feelings of warmth as well as tenderness in describing its cuteness.

Have you had any experience with the "kawaii culture"? Or maybe you are interested in immersing yourself in this experience?

If you would like to experience "kawaii fashion", a place called Harajuku would be the best to visit. You will most definitely meet someone dressed in "kawaii fashion" on the street, and you will find many shops with themes of "kawaii items". You will even find food that it is a "kawaii" version, for example cotton candy, waffles, etc.

If you are a little less interested in "kawaii culture" itself, and are more interested in "Anime", your go-to place is most definitely the famous Akihabara - the sanctuary of anime geeks, who are known as "オタク"(otaku). And to keep everyone included, Ghibli fans - you will not want to miss the Ghibli Museum in Mitaka. Everyone has a place to visit for their area of interest!

CHAPTER 4:

Numbers and Time: Expanding your statement !

Numbers. Definitely one of the most important things to master when it comes to studying a new language. Knowing the numbers makes it easy to state the time, the date, as well as describe specific quantities, which are all necessary and useful skills.

4.1 One to Ninety Nine

Let's get started by learning the 10 most important numbers in Japanese.

Yes, we only need to learn 10 numbers and we can state One to Ninety Nine!

And these 10 numbers, believe it or not, is all you'll need to know in order to tell the time in Japanese — no need to overwhelm yourself with learning how to count into the hundreds or thousands.

Numbers 1 to 10

1	ichi (いち)
2	ni　 (に)
3	san (さん)
4	yon / shi (よん/ し)
5	go (ご)
6	roku (ろく)
7	nana / shichi (なな/ しち)
8	hachi (はち)
9	ku /kyū (く/ きゅう)
10	jū　(じゅう)

Since Japanese uses a number stacking system, it is just a matter of adding these numbers to express bigger numbers. For example, the number 22. The number 22 is made up of two tens, and one two – i.e. 10 + 10 + 2 = 22. And that is essentially how you would say the number in Japanese: two-ten-two.

11	jūichi (じゅういち)
12	jūni (じゅうに)
13	jūsan (じゅう さん)
20	nijū (にじゅう)
25	nijū go (にじゅう ご)
30	sanjū (さん じゅう)
40	yonjū (よん じゅう)
50	gojū (ごじゅう)
90	kyūjū (きゅう じゅう)
100	hyaku (ひゃく)

This is how numbers are called after the number 10:

→ Notice that 11 is called ten-one; 'jū' is ten, and 'ichi' is one. Put them together and you get 11!

→ Here we have 25, two-ten-five; 'ni' is two, 'jū' is ten, and 'go' is five. Put them together and you create nijū go!

4.2 What time is it? / Nanji desu ka?

Now that we've got a hold of the numbers in Japanese, it is the perfect transition into telling time! It is an essential part of our daily lives to be able to tell the time.

Telling the time in Japanese is quite straightforward as it follows a very simple format. The suffix for hours or o'clock is "ji" (じ), and for minute is "fun" (ふん) or "pun" (ぷん). When telling the time, you will *always* mentioned the suffix "ji" (じ).

Let's take one example. Say the time is 5:15 (a.m. or p.m. is irrelevant to this point).

In English, you may say "It is five-fifteen", and one would understand the time. However, in Japanese, you would not simply say the numbers. You will *always* attach the suffix "ji" (じ) to the hour. So, in Japanese, 5:15 would be, "go ji jūgo fun" (ごじ じゅうご ふん). The "ji" (じ) after the "go" (ご) has to be included.

Learn Time-related Words

Now let's get into the time-related words besides "ji" (じ) and "fun" (ふん) or "pun" (ぷん). Here are some words you'll need to know to tell time.

Rōmaji	Hiragana	Meaning
ji	じ	o'clock
fun / pun	ふん / ぷん	minute
gozen	ごぜん	a.m.
gogo	ごご	p.m.
han	はん	half (half past)

When you state the time, remember that the words for a.m. or p.m. come before the time. For example, expressing 8 p.m. would be "gogo hachi ji" (ごご はち じ). The "gogo" (ごご) expresses that it is in the p.m., and is mentioned *before* the actual time.

Example Usage

Some more examples we can look at:

- 5:30 a.m. is "gozen go ji han" (ごぜん ごじ はん). Once again, the "gozen" (ごぜん) to represent the a.m. is written before the actual time. Here we also use "han" (はん) to express that it is half-past the mentioned hour. You are more than welcome to say the number itself. If so, it would be "gozen go ji sanjuppun" (ごぜん　ごじ　さんじゅっぷん)

- 7:00 p.m. is "gogo shichi ji" (ごご しちじ). As always, keeping the "gogo" (ごご) in the beginning, and then proceeding to express the hour.

There are a few exceptions to take note of when telling time, and these pertain to the numbers 4, 7, and 9.

A quick glance back at how to say these numbers will show that the numbers 4, 7, and 9, are "yon" (よん), "nana" (なな), and "kyu" (きゅう). However, when expressing 4:00, there is a *slight* change that occurs. When you would like to express 4:00, you would say, "yo-ji" (よじ) – the 'n' of 'yon' is removed. When expressing time, you will *only* express 4:00 in this way. As for 7:00 and 9:00, you simply need to be aware of which pronunciation you use. In the table above, you will have seen two ways of pronouncing these numbers. Just ensure that when telling the time, you use "shichi" (しち) for 7, and "ku" (く) for 9! It would be *incorrect* to say 'nana-ji' or 'kyu-ji'.

Let's see all the hours of the day in one table:

1:00	ichi-ji (いち じ)
2:00	ni-ji (に じ)
3:00	san-ji (さん じ)
4:00	yo-ji (よ じ)
5:00	go-ji (ご じ)
6:00	raku-ji (ろく じ)
7:00	shichi-ji (しち じ)
8:00	hachi-ji (はち じ)
9:00	ku-ji (く じ)
10:00	jū-ji (じゅう じ)
11:00	jūichi-ji (じゅういち じ)
12:00	jūni-ji (じゅうに じ)

Minute

This part might be quite a confusing part to learn. The usage of "fun" (ふん) or "pun" (ぷん) does not seem to follow a set of rules, neither does it have a set pattern. Let's take a look:

:01	ippun (いっぷん)
:02	ni fun (にふん)
:03	san pun (さんぷん)
:04	yon pun (よんぷん)
:05	go fun (ごふん)
:06	roppun (ろっぷん)
:07	nana fun (ななふん)
:08	happun (はっぷん)
:09	kyū fun (きゅうふん)
:10	juppun (じゅっぷん)
:11	jūippun (じゅういっぷん)
:12	jūni fun (じゅうにふん)

But, the good news is that we don't necessarily have to be so precise about each minute when telling the time. As long as you are familiar with how to say each 5-minute interval, you will be well understood in conversation.

Time	fun (ふん)	pun (ぷん)
1:05	ichi-ji gofun	
1:10		ichi-ji juppun
1:15	ichi-ji jūgofun	
1:20		ichi-ji nijuppun
1:25	ichi-ji nijūgofun	
1:30		ichi-ji sanjuppun / ichi-ji han
1:35	ichi-ji sanjūgofun	
1:40		ichi-ji yonjuppun
1:45	ichi-ji yonjūgofun	
1:50		ichi-ji gojuppun
1:55	ichi-ji gojūgofun	

With the 5-minute intervals, you may be able to notice the pattern. As beneficial as it is to know the expression for each minute, in reality, studying the pattern of these 5-minute intervals is a good place to start.

☑Check list #5

Can you state the time below?

☐3:40

☐4:50 am

☐7:30

☐8:25pm

☐9:45am

4.3 How much is it? Numbers from 100 onwards

Numbers 100 to 900:

Numbers	Rōmaji	Hiragana
100	hyaku	ひゃく
200	ni nyaku	にひゃく
300	san byaku	さんびゃく
400	yon hyaku	よんひゃく
500	go hyaku	ごひゃく
600	roppyaku	ろっぴゃく
700	nana hyaku	ななひゃく
800	happyaku	はっぴゃく
900	kyu hyaku	きゅうひゃく

Numbers 1000 to 9000:

Numbers	Rōmaji	Hiragana
1,000	sen	せん
2,000	ni sen	にせん
3,000	san zen	さんぜん
4,000	yon sen	よんせん
5,000	go sen	ごせん
6,000	roku sen	ろくせん

7,000	nana sen	ななせん
8,000	hassen	はっせん
9,000	kyu sen	きゅうせん

Japanese currency has a unit of 10,000 as well, which is called "man" (まん). Luckily, unlike the 100's and 1000's, there are no exceptions in pronunciation.

Numbers	Rōmaji	Hiragana
10,000	ichi man	いちまん
20,000	ni man	にまん
30,000	san man	さんまん
40,000	yon man	よんまん
50,000	go man	ごまん
60,000	roku man	ろくまん
70,000	nana man	ななまん
80,000	hachi man	はちまん
90,000	kyu man	きゅうまん

The Japanese currency unit (¥) is called "yen", however the sound of "y" is not pronounced and we say "en". The symbol " ¥ " is always placed before the numbers such as " ¥ 150". When reading / saying prices, the number itself is read first, and then the "en" comes after. For example, " ¥ 150" is read as "hyaku go jū en" (ひゃく ごじゅう えん).

☑Check list #6

Can you say these prices?

☐ ¥ 1200

☐ ¥ 13000

☐ ¥ 8600

☐ ¥ 335

☐ ¥ 890

4.4 Name of the month and Days of the Week

As you are already familiar with numbers in Japanese, you'll be able to learn the names of the months easily.

Knowing numbers from one to ten is all you need to name all the months.

Rōmaji	Hiragana	Kanji	English
ichi gatsu	いちがつ	一月	January
ni gatsu	にがつ	二月	February
san gatsu	さんがつ	三月	March
shi gatsu	しがつ	四月	April
go gatsu	ごがつ	五月	May
roku gatsu	ろくがつ	六月	June
shichi gatsu	しちがつ	七月	July
hachi gatsu	はちがつ	八月	August
ku gatsu	くがつ	九月	September
jū gatsu	じゅうがつ	十月	October

Rōmaji	Hiragana	Kanji	English
ichi gatsu	いちがつ	一月	January
jūichi gatsu	じゅういちがつ	十一月	November
jūni gatsu	じゅうにがつ	十二月	December

Days of the Week

Learning the days of the week can be easy as well, since each word for the days of the week ends with the same suffix, which is "yōbi".

Rōmaji	Hiragana	Kanji	English
nichi yōbi	にちようび	日曜日	Sunday
getsu yōbi	げつようび	月曜日	Monday
ka yōbi	かようび	火曜日	Tuesday
sui yōbi	すいようび	水曜日	Wednesday
moku yōbi	もくようび	木曜日	Thursday
kin yōbi	きんようび	金曜日	Friday
do yōbi	どようび	土曜日	Saturday

Remembering the Days of the Week with Kanji

The above list of the Names of the Week includes the Kanji description as well.

We talked about the Kanji in Chapter 1, but never delved deeper into it. Perhaps it is time that we weave the study of Kanji into the things we are learning. Though you may be daunted by the thought of studying Kanji, especially when you're just beginning, let's give these few Kanji characters a chance!

The first Kanji character for each day of the week represents an element of nature. Those characters of Kanji are very simple and most of them are hieroglyphic, meaning they are of pictographic origin.

As mentioned earlier, each day ends with the same suffix, which is "ようび ・ 曜日" (yōbi). So really, when it comes to learning the Kanji for the days of week, it is only the first character that you will need to pay close attention to. Let's delve into each day, and maybe you'll see how useful Kanji is!

Nichi yōbi (Sunday) 日

The Kanji "日" (nichi) literally means "sun" or "day".

This simple shape of Kanji is believed to symbolize the representation of the sunrise, where the horizontal line presents the horizon. Over the years, the circular shape of the sun was simplified and stylized into a rectangular shape, resulting in the current shape of 日.

Remember that Kanji characters can be read in several ways. 日 can be read as "hi" (ひ), "ka" (か), "bi" (び), or "nichi" (にち).

Getsu yōbi (Monday) 月

The Kanji of 月 (getsu) means "moon". It can be read as "getsu" (げつ), "gatsu" (がつ) and "tsuki" (つき) depending on the context. This shape of 月 is considered to be a pictograph of a crescent moon. Considering 'Monday' has been also known as 'Moonday', it would be easy to remember that the Kanji for Monday is that of the moon!

Ka yōbi (Tuesday) 火

This Kanji for 火 (ka) means "fire". 火 can also be read as "ka" (か) and "hi" (ひ).The character originally depicted the flames of a fire and gradually evolved into its modern form. Can you imagine the flaming fire with this character?

Sui yōbi (Wednesday) 水

This Kanji for 水 (sui) means "water". Similar to 火 (ka), this character originally depicted water flowing from a mountain. The eventual modifications and simplifications led to its current form.

If you have remembered 火曜日 (ka yōbi), the element of fire, you can connect it to the next day 水曜日 (sui yōbi), the element of water, by imagining a fire being put out by water.

Moku yōbi (Thursday) 木

This Kanji for 木 (moku) means "tree". It can be read as "ki" (き) as well.

The character depicts a tree as easily imagined as the shape of the tree with branches stood up firmly on the ground.

Kin yōbi (Friday) 金

The meaning of this Kanji 金 (kin) is "gold". It is easy enough to remember this character, since Friday is golden for everyone, right? We all look forward Fridays, because we are *ready* for the weekend! This Kanji for 金 (kin) can also be read as "kane" (かね) which means "money" in Japanese.

Do yōbi (Saturday) 土

Saturday is finally here! The Kanji for 土 (do) means "earth", "ground", or "soil". Again this character is a pictogram, a character that represents the physical shape of the Earth with mounds of soil and stones.

This Kanji character of 土 can be pronounced in several ways depending on the context. Beside "do" (ど), it reads as "tsuchi" (つち) which means "soil" in Japanese.

Hopefully learning the days of the week in Japanese isn't as hard as it looks. Now that we've seen the connection of each day to an element, are you starting to think that Kanji could actually be interesting? Or, perhaps maybe even start to feel a slight appreciation for the help it can provide?

4.5 Other Japanese Words related to Days and Dates

In addition to the days of the week, we will look at a few more words and phrases related to the calendar.

Rōmaji	Hiragana	Kanji	Meaning
kyō	きょう	今日	Today
ashita	あした	明日	Tomorrow
asatte	あさって	明後日	The day after tomorrow
kinō	きのう	昨日	Yesterday
ototoi	おととい	一昨日	The day before yesterday
shū	しゅう	週	Week
konshū	こんしゅう	今週	This week
raishū	らいしゅう	来週	Next week
senshū	せんしゅう	先週	Last week
tsuki, gatsu	つき、がつ	月	Month
kongetsu	こんげつ	今月	This Month
raigetsu	らいげつ	来月	Next Month
sengetsu	せんげつ	先月	Last Month
toshi, nen	とし	年	Year
kotoshi	ことし	今年	This year
rainen	らいねん	来年	Next year
sakunen, kyonen	さくねん、きょねん	昨年、去年	Last year

You may notice some patterns of the same kanji being used. For example, 今 of 今日 (きょう), 今 of 今週 (こんしゅう), and 今 of 今年 (ことし) are same.

This kanji word of 今 refers to the present, while 来 refers to the future. By knowing this it may be simple to link it to the Kanji for 'year' or 'month', to create your desired word.

Although it may be difficult to remember or memorize all the kanji words, just by recognizing some of them will be helpful in understanding certain contexts.

Example Usage & Exercises

Using date related words, and some adjectives. Let's try to form some sentences.

- Raishu wa isogashii desu. (らいしゅう は いそがしい です。)

- Hachi gatsu wa atsui desu. (はちがつ は あつい です。)

- Ni gatsu wa samui desu. (にがつ は さむい です。)

Could you understand the meaning of the sentences? Let's look at each sentence:

- Raishū wa isogashii desu.⇨ " I will be busy next week."
- Hachi gatsu wa atsui desu. ⇨ " It is hot in August."
- Ni gatsu wa samui desu. ⇨ " It is cold in February."

Days of the Month

Saying the days of the months in Japanese is a little bit more complicated than the names of the months or days of the week as there are a few rules to follow.

The basic pattern for the days and date is: number (date) + "NICHI" (にち・ 日). All the dates are written in this pattern either with Kanji or with Arabic numbers. However, when it comes to reading, there are some exceptions and irregularities.

The days, especially those from one to ten, are unique as their way of reading is the remnants of the ancient ways of counting numbers in Japanese.

From the 11th day to the end of a month, we say the corresponding number and add NICHI, which means "a day." SO, for example, the 11th day is "jūichi nichi" (じゅう いち にち). There are only three exceptions to keep in mind: the 14th, the 20th, and the 24th.

To make it easy to grasp the days of the month, below are all 31 days of the month.

Rōmaji	Hiragana	Kanji	English
tsuitachi	ついたち	一日	1st
futsuka	ふつか	二日	2nd
mikka	みっか	三日	3rd
yokka	よっか	四日	4th
itsuka	いつか	五日	5th
muika	むいか	六日	6th
nanoka	なのか	七日	7th
yōka	ようか	八日	8th
kokonoka	ここのか	九日	9th
tōka	とおか	十日	10th
jūichi nichi	じゅういち　にち	十一日	11th
jūni nichi	じゅうに　にち	十二日	12th
jūsan nichi	じゅうさん　にち	十三日	13th
jū yokka	じゅう　よっか	十四日	14th
jūgo nichi	じゅうご　にち	十五日	15th
jūroku nichi	じゅうろく　にち	十六日	16th
jūshichi nichi	じゅうしち　にち	十七日	17th
jūhachi nichi	じゅうはち　にち	十八日	18th

jūku nichi	じゅうく　にち	十九日	19th
hatsuka	はつか	二十日	20th
nijū ichi nichi	にじゅういち　にち	二十一日	21th
nijū ni nichi	にじゅうに　にち	二十二日	22th
nijū san nichi	にじゅうさん　にち	二十三日	23th
nijū yokka	にじゅう　よっか	二十四日	24th
nijū go nichi	にじゅうご　にち	二十五日	25th
nijū roku nichi	にじゅうろく　にち	二十六日	26th
nijū shichi nichi	にじゅうしち　にち	二十七日	27th
nijū hachi nichi	にじゅうはち　にち	二十八日	28th
nijū ku nichi	にじゅうく　にち	二十九日	29th
sanjū nichi	さんじゅう　にち	三十日	30th
sanjū ichi nichi	さんじゅういち　にち	三十一日	31th

You should have noticed that the first 10 days have a special way of reading, and does not follow the date + "nichi" (にち) rule. Then you will have seen the exceptions of the 14th and 24th, whereby there is no inclusion of "nichi" (にち), and the 20th that is another unique way of reading!

When the date is in full, the order is: YEAR / MONTH / DAY. So it would like to express a date in 2023, it would be:

2023 nen 11 gatsu 13 nichi

2023 年 11 月 13 日.

Exercise 4

Read the sentence and check that you understand the meaning.

1. Kyō wa getsuyōbi desu. (きょう は げつようび です。)

2. 10 gatsu 31 nichi wa kayōbi desu. (１０がつ３１にち は かようび です。)

3. Konshū wa hima desu. (こんしゅう は ひま です。)

☑Check list #7

Can you say these phrases in Japanese?

☐ "One to ten"

☐ "What time is it?

☐ "It is 4 o'clock"

☐ "Today is Tuesday."

☐ "Tomorrow will be December 31st."

Nihongo Trivia

~HACHI is a lucky number~

The number "8" is considered to be a lucky number in Japan.

The reason for this lies in the shape of the Kanji "hachi".

The Kanji for "Hachi" is "八" where both strokes are spreading out wide as it moves down towards the bottom of the character. The spreading from "top" (present) to "down" (future), implies prosperity and eternal development. This is what makes this number so lucky!

On the contrary, people tend to avoid numbers "four" and "nine". Number "four" is pronounced as "shi" (し) which is the same pronunciation as "death". "Nine" is pronounced as " ku" (く) which means "suffering".

On weddings or other special occasions, even numbers are avoided. Since even numbers can be divided, it is believed to be bad luck as it could imply a separation. Only the number "hachi" is the exception as it is believed to bring prosperity and eternal development. So when it comes to these special occasions, ensure that the number of the gifts to wrap, or to the number of the course to a meal, are *not* "2", "4", or "6"!

CHAPTER 5:

Demonstrative & Question Words / Expressing Likes and dislikes

Kosoado words (こそあど ことば / こそあど言葉) are the series of demonstrative pronouns words - these words are, "this", "that", "here", and "there". They can be used to refer to things, people, locations based on the physical distance between the speaker and the listener.

In this chapter, along with KOSOADO words, we are going to cover interrogative words such as wh-words – i.e. "who", "what", "when", "where", and "why" – and we will learn how to express likes and dislikes in Japanese.

5.1 Basic of KOSOADO words

As mentioned earlier, "kosoado" words are words such as this" and 'that" or "here" and "there" in English. Although in English these words tend to come in pairs, in Japanese, each set is made up of three words starting with "ko", "so", and "a". Plus a corresponding questioning word starting with "do". Each set of four words begins with these characters. This is the reason these words are called Kosoado words (こそあど ことば/ こそあど言葉).

For example, the equivalent of "this" in Japanese is "kore" (これ) , and "that" is "sore" (それ),

There is another word "are" (あれ) which means "that one over there". Each set has a corresponding question word that begins with "do", such as "dore" which means "which one".

Knowing these KOSOADO words, your descriptions are expanding tremendously.

	Things (abstract /+ noun)	Place	Direction	Manner
ko	*KORE / KONO* + noun	KOKO	KOCHIRA	KONNA
so	SORE / SONO + noun	SOKO	SOCHIRA	SONNA
a	ARE / ANO + noun	ASOKO	ACHIRA	ANNA
do	DORE /DONO + noun	DOKO	DOCHIRA	DONNA

THE BASICS of KOSOADO

KORE (this), KOKO (here, at this place), KOCHIRA (this way) and KONNA (like this) belong to the KO group, as all of these words begin with KO. They all refer to things, people or places close to the speaker.

SORE (it), SOKO (there), SOCHIRA(that way) and SONNA(like that) belong to the SO group. These words refer to things, people, or places close to the listener. But if the speaker and the listener are close together, let's say side by side, these words can refer to things , places or people a little distant from both of them.

ARE (that), ASOKO (over there) and ANNA (like that)belong to the A group. These are the words for things, places, or people distant from both the speaker and the listener.

And DORE (which), DOKO (where) and DONNA (what kind of) are in the DO group. These are words for interrogative sentences.

✦ Quick Review ✦

☆ KO-words: Words that begin with "ko" (こ) are used for things that are relatively close to the speaker, or closer than to the speaker that to the listener.

☆ SO-words: Words that with so "so" (そ) are used for referring things that are further from the speaker and / or are closer to the listener.

☆ A-words: Words that begin with "a" (あ) are used for things that are far from both the speaker and the listener.

☆ DO-words: Words that begin with do "do" (ど) are used to ask a question.

☑Check list #8

Can you say these phrases in Japanese?

☐ "Here"

☐ "Where"

☐ "This one"

☐ "That one is cheap."

☐ "This is delicious."

5.2 Basic of Question words

We can build upon our knowledge of "kosoado" words by integrating it with question words. Since we have learned how to describe "here" and "there", we can build upon it by learning how to ask the question that would initiate such a response – i.e. "where is it?".

Let's take a look at what is known as the wh- words in English:

English	Rōmaji	hiragana
what	nani/ nan	なに/ なん
where	doko	どこ
who	dare	だれ
when	itsu	いつ
why	doushite/ naze	どうして/ なぜ
how	dou	どう

These are the 6 question words in Japanese. Let's dive deeper into using each one!

Along with this questioning words of interrogative sentences, we build some vocabularies so that we can expand our skills of forming sentences as well as understanding the spoken languages. We will be using these for the example sentences below.

English	Rōmaji	Hiragana
now	ima	いま
birthday	tanjō bi	たんじょうび
appointment	yoyaku	よやく
hotel	hoteru	ホテル

toilet	toire	トイレ
museum	bijutsu kan	びじゅつかん
cuisine/meal	ryori	りょうり
sports	supōtsu	スポーツ
trip / travelling	ryokō	りょこう

5.3 Questions using What

Asking questions with the word "nani / nan" (なに / なん) can be most frequently used from the questions such as "What is it?" "What is that?" or "What time is it now?" to "What day of the week is it today?". To start creating more varied sentences, we will be using the vocabulary from the table above. We can use these vocabularies to pieces together and create questions using "nani / nan" (なに / なん).

Example Usage

- Kore wa nan desu ka?

  o これ は なん です か。

  o Meaning: What is this?

- Sore wa nan desu ka?

  o それ は なん です か。

  o Meaning: What is that?

- Ima nanji desu ka?

  o いま なんじ です か。

  o Meaning: What time is it now?

- Kyō wa nan yōbi desu ka?

- きょうは なんようび です か。

  - Meaning: What day of the week is it today?

- Kyō wa nan gatsu nan nichi desu ka?

  - きょうは なんがつ なんにち ですか。

  - Meaning: What date is it today?

- Otanjōbi wa nan gatsu nan nichi desu ka?

  - おたんじょうび は なんがつ なんにち ですか。

  - Meaning: When is your birthday?

- Yoyaku wa nan nichi desuka ?

  - よやく は なんにち ですか。

  - Meaning: When is the reservation?

You may have noticed the use of "なんがつ なんにち" (nan gatsu nan nichi) in these sentences. This literally means, "what month, what date". And although when written in this manner, it does become a "what" question, this phrase is another way of expressing "when" in Japanese! You may be thinking, "why not just use "いつ" (itsu) to ask when something is?". You are most definitely allowed to use "いつ" (itsu) for asking "when" questions, but it is always nice to know a another way of asking!

5.4 Questions using Where

"doko" (どこ) is a pronoun that is a part of the KOSOADO words that we just learned, and it is the equivalent to "where" in English. When you use it in a sentence, we place the topic / noun first. Here are some examples:

Example Usage

- Hoteru wa doko desuka?

  - ホテル は どこ ですか。

- o Meaning: Where is the hotel?

- Toire wa doko desuka?

  - o トイレ は どこ です か。

  - o Meaning: Where is the toilet?

- Bijutsu kan wa doko desuka?

  - o びじゅつかん は どこ です か。

  - o Meaning: Where is the museum?

5.5 Questions using who

"だれ" (dare) can be used in a sentence such as "who is that?" But this word is more frequent in the verb sentences to ask who does that action. "dare" (だれ) often joins with particles like "no" (の) or "to" (と) to indicate of "whose" or "with whom".

Particle "no" (の) indicates possession, and joins noun to noun; therefore, putting "dare" (だれ)) and "no" (の) together forms "dare no" (だれの), which means "whose".

Example Usage

- Are wa dare desuka?

  - o あれ は だれ です か。

  - o Meaning: Who is that?

- Kore wa dare no desuka?

  - o これ は だれの です か。

  - o Meaning: Whose is this?

- Kyou wa dare no tanjōbi desuka?

  - o きょう は だれの たんじょうび です か。

o   Meaning: Whose birthday is it today?

✦ Did you get all the sentences formed correctly?

If you start having problems forming the sentence, keep in mind the sentence pattern (<u>topic wa noun desu</u>) and make sure we bring out the topic first. ✦

5.6 Questions using when

As mentioned in the section of 5.3, "itsu" can be replaced by "nan gatsu nan nichi" or any word questioning the date. Just have a quick review of the sentences, "when is your birthday? And "when is the reservation" using "itsu".

Example Usage

- Otanjōbi wa itsu desuka?

  o   おたんじょうび は いつ ですか。

  o   Meaning: When is your birthday?

- Yoyaku wa itsu desuka?

  o   よやく は いつ ですか。

  o   Meaning: When is the reservation?

If you are talking to someone, we do not need to place the word "you" (あなた) as it is obvious that we are asking the birthday of the person whom you are talking to. We speak more on this in Chapter 6.2, in the "avoiding the repetition" section.

5.7 Likes and Dislikes

The Japanese words to express "likes and dislikes" are actually na-adjectives. This is different from English as "like" and "dislike" are both considered to be verbs.

The word for "like" is "sukina" (すきな) and the one for "dislike" is "kiraina" (きらいな).

How do we use these words to express our feelings in a sentence? We'll do this by looking back at sentence patterns.

(topic) wa noun ga suki desu.
(topic) は noun　が　すきです。
<u>meaning: (Subject) likes noun.</u>

(topic) wa noun ga kirai desu
(topic) は noun　が　きらいです。
<u>meaning: (topic) dislikes noun.</u>

Here one of the most important point to take note is:

The particle "ga" (が) is always used *before* the either the word "suki"(すき) or "kirai"(きらい).

We are already aware that "suki"(すき) and "kirai"(きらい) are both na-adjectives, and thus making negative sentences can be done by following the rules that we learned.

(topic) wa noun ga suki dewaarimasen.
(topic) は noun　が　すきではありません。
<u>meaning: (Subject) does not like noun.</u>

(topic) wa noun ga kirai desu
(topic) は noun　が　きらいではありません。
<u>meaning: (topic) does not dislike noun.</u>

Example Usage

- Watashi wa *dōbutsu ga suki desu.

  ○ わたし は どうぶつ が すき です。

- o   Meaning: I like * animals.

- Watashi wa *shokubutsu ga suki desu.

    o   わたし は しょくぶつ が すきです。

    o   Meaning: I like * plants.

- Imōto wa benkyō ga kirai desu.

    o   いもうと は べんきょう が きらい です。

    o   Meaning: My younger sister does not like to study.

- Haha wa anime ga kirai desu.

    o   はは は アニメ が きらい です。

    o   Meaning: My mother dislikes anime.

5.8 Questions about likes and dislikes

In the section of KOSOADO words, we learned "donna" which means "what kind of". With this word, "donna" we can ask someone more challenging questions like "what kind of sports do you like?" or "what kind of cuisine/ meals do you like?" Are you ready?

Example Usage

- Donna supōtsu ga suki desu ka?

    o   どんな スポーツ が すき です か。

    o   Meaning: What kind of sports do you like?

- Donna ryōri ga suki desu ka?

    o   どんな りょうりが すき です か。

    o   Meaning: What kind of dish / cuisine do you like?

Are you starting to get the hang of making sentences in Japanese? You can practice creating question sentences and responses with this list of sports!

English	Rōmaji	Hiragana / katakana
baseball	yakyū	やきゅう
swimming	suiei	すいえい
jūdō	jūdō	じゅうどう
karate	karate	からて
Tennis	tenisu	テニス
golf	gorufu	ゴルフ
soccer	sakkā	サッカー
skating	sukēto	スケート
volleyball	barēbōruu	バレーバール
basketball	basukettobōru	バスケットボール

☑Check list #9

Can you say these phrases or words in Japanese?

□ "I like travelling."

□ "Who"

□ "When"

□ "What kind of"

□ "I do not like golf"

Nihongo Trivia

Does そう (sō) ＝ so !?

One of the meanings of the Japanese word "そう" (sō) is very similar to the English word "so".

If you want to express "it is so", we san say "sō desu" (そう です).

Let's look at some more versions with this interesting "so".

"sō desu ka?" = is that so?

"sō desu ne." = it is so, that's right

"sō desu yo." = it is so, that's right

"Ne" is used to express the assurance or confirmation, while "yo" is placed when the speaker needs to convey a message that the listener does not know of. It is more assertive, while 'ne' is more friendly and in agreement to what is being said. Note that the simple phrase of confirmation "sō desu" could sound abrupt, which is often why "yo" or "ne" would be added.

There is a joke among beginner Japanese learners that when you do not understand a conversation, you can just keep saying, "sō desu ne." or "sō desu ka?". Although it may be a joke, it is true that the conversation will continue if you reply with those phrases, as you are simply showing agreement to or interest in the topic of conversation!

CHAPTER 6:

Uniqueness of Japanese Language

Over the last 5 chapters, we have progressed a lot in stating and forming sentences with nouns and adjectives. Before we move onto even more sentence-learning, let's take a slight break here to discuss cultural characteristics of the Japanese language.

The Japanese language is unique in many ways. You may have noticed a few features as you studied the writing systems and word orders. We will look at a few characteristics that differentiate Japanese from other languages – namely through particles, and the use of honorifics.

6.1 Japanese Particles

Though particles might just be a small fragment of a sentence, they are vital and play a significant role. Particles give meaning to a word more than its place in the sentence does. The most important rule is that the particles always follow the word they're modifying.

Japanese sentences are often explained as using a SOV (Subject Object Verb) formula, which is different from the English SVO (Subject Verb Object) structure. Simply applying the formula of SOV (Subject Object Verb) may not necessarily lead to the creation of a comprehensive sentence. Unfortunately, the SOV structure is not enough to explain the order in which we write Japanese sentences. This is because particles determine even the function of the phrase. As a result, we need to break up sentences into segments of "word" and "particle". If you would like an explanation using the formula, the closest way to describe the Japanese sentence may be the SPOPV formula: (Subject Particle + Object Particle + Verb).

Seeing how crucial particles are, knowing and perfecting the usage of the particles is a key to accurate sentences. So far, we have learned the particles "wa" (は) "ga" (が) "mo" (も) "no" (の) "to" (と);

not only is there a wide variety of particles, but they sometimes also have more than one usage. Let's summarize the particles that we learned so far as well as the particles to be learned in the next few chapters.

Here we briefly look at some particles and their roles.

- は (wa) is attached to the topic of the sentence/ <u>topic marker</u>

- も (mo) is used to express the <u>meaning of "also"</u>

- が (ga) is attached to <u>the subject of the sentence</u>, emphasizing the subject when there is more than one topic

- と (to) is used to express <u>the meaning of "with", as well as " and"</u>

- を (o) is attached to <u>the direct object of the sentence/ object marker</u> – we are going to learn this in chapter 7.

- で (de) is attached to either <u>the means / method </u>of a verb or the <u>location</u> of the action taking place

- に (ni) is attached to the word to indicate <u>the time or destination or direction </u>that verb takes place.

- から (kara) is to indicate the <u>starting point of the time or space</u>

- まで (made) is to indicate the <u>finishing point of the time or space</u>

- の (no) <u>possession</u>

- の (no) <u>as noun modifier</u>

Particle "no" is extremely useful as its role is a way to turn a noun into a modifier.

Generally, "no" can turn any noun into a modifier, regardless of whether it has any ownership over anything. Often the function of "no" is referred to the English preposition "of", which you would simply join two nouns – i.e. "expression of possession". For example, A no B / "nihongo no hon" (にほんご の ほん) means "japanese book" or "raishū no getsu yōbi"(らいしゅう の げつようび) means "next week Monday" and so on.

There are many more particles as well as more usages for each particle than the list has mentioned. It is best to learn / remember each particle together with a sentence pattern. From the next chapter, we are going to learn various sentence patterns including verb sentences – it becomes especially important to focus on which particles are present when looking at verb sentences!

Fun fact: there is actually no limit to the number of "no" (の) that you can have in a single sentence. Take a look at this sentence:

Watashi no tomodachi no okāsan no nihongo no gakkō no sensei no ie wa koko desu.

わたし の ともだち の おかあさん の にほんご の がっこう の せんせい の いえ は

ここ です。

Although it may look daunting, if we simply segment parts of the sentence and look at it with its particle, the sentence becomes so much easier to understand! Breaking this sentence up will lead to:

わたし の /ともだち の /おかあさん の /にほんご の /がっこう の /せんせい の/ いえ は

ここ です。

Maybe it is a little easier to understand the meaning of this sentence now? The sentence means: "My friend's mother's Japanese school teacher's house is here." The same sentence could also be written as:

Koko wa watashi no tomodachi no okāsan no nihongo no gakkō no sensei no ie desu.

ここは わたし の /ともだち の /おかあさん の /にほんご の /がっこう の /

せんせい の /いえ です。

Although we were speaking mainly of how important particles are within a sentence, we can also see how *useful* it is as it almost acts as a guide to our understanding.

☑Check list #10

Can you say these phrases or words in Japanese?

☐ "From Monday to Friday"

☐ "Next week Saturday"

☐ "Me too"

☐ "Japanese book"

☐ "My friend's mother"

6.2 honorifics

One of the most important parts of Japanese culture is *being polite*, and this is directly reflected in the honorifics of the language. There is a huge misunderstanding and misinformation regarding honorifics in Japanese, especially by the materials written in English. This misinformation leads to a culture being wrongly presented. The misunderstanding is caused mainly by looking at only one portion of the grammar rules. Here, we will look at the entirety of honorifics to properly grasp its concept.

Honorifics are called KEIGO (けいご・ 敬語) in Japanese, and this can be divided into 3 groups:

1. Respectful form – "Sonkei-go" (そんけいご・ 尊敬語))

2. Humble form – "kenjō- go" (けんじょうご・謙譲語)

3. Polite form – "teinei- go" (ていねいご・ 丁寧語)

"Sonkei-go" (そんけいご) is used when referring to the action of the person you are talking to, while the "kenjō-go" (けんじょうご) is used to refer to your own actions – a way of humbling yourself. Another way of understanding the difference between the two is to think of "sonkei-go" (そんけいご) as a means of raising the level of importance of the person you are speaking to, while the "kenjō-go" (けんじょうご) is a way of lowering the importance of your own actions. Both methods are meant to show respect towards the person that you are speaking to.

SONKEI-GO (そんけいご・ 尊敬語)

"Sonkei-go" is used when speaking to and referring to the actions of someone of a higher position – i.e. a superior at work, a client, etc. What happens when using this form is that the verb of the sentence changes into a more polite form. In some cases, the verb will change completely. This is a tough topic to comprehend, so let's look at it through examples.

Upon entering a shop or restaurant in Japan, you will be welcomed by staff saying "irasshaimase" (いらっしゃいませ). This is a very common phrase, and you will most likely be hearing it for the majority of your visit to Japan. This is a greeting in "Sonkei-go" form, meaning it is a form of welcoming you – the customer – with respect as you enter your place of choice. If "irasshaimase" (いらっしゃいませ) is the "Sonkei-go" form, what was the original verb form?

The word "irasshaimase" (いらっしゃいませ) derives from the verb "kimasu" (きます), which means "to come" or "to enter". This verb, "kimasu" is the original verb, which is then changed to "irasshaimasu" (いらっしゃいます), that is the "Sonkei-go" form. You may be thinking, "irasshaimasu" (いらっしゃいます) and "irasshaimase" (いらっしゃいませ) look different. And you're right. "Irassaimasu" (いらっしゃいます) is the "Sonkei-go" verb form, but in order for this to be a greeting to someone, it would be changed to "irassaimase" (いらっしゃいませ). It may be a bit tricky to understand, but this is just one example of how verbs are changed to create "Sonkei-go" form.

KENJŌ-GO (けんじょうご・謙譲語)

The purpose of "Kenjō-go" is to lower yourself or your social status when speaking about your own actions. It should be used when you're speaking to someone of higher social status when describing an action of yours or someone of your circle. Like "Sonkeigo", "Kenjō-go" words can also take the form of a changed verb, or a different verb completely.

One example of "Kenjo-go" is the phrase "itadakimasu" (いただきます). This is a form of greeting before starting a meal. The original verb is "moraimasu" (もらいます), which means "to receive" or "to accept". In order to humble our action of receiving a meal or a drink, we would say the phrase "itadakimasu" (いただきます). Once again, we can see how the original verb and the "Kenjo-go" form verb are noticeably different.

TEINEI-GO (ていねいご・ 丁寧語)

The word "teinei" (ていねい) means "polite", which explains why "Teinei-go" literally means "polite form". Of the three groups of Honorifics / KEIGO (けいご・ 敬語), "Teineigo" is the easiest and most commonly observed. It is usually the first form of Honorifics / KEIGO (けいご・ 敬語) that is taught to students. In fact you have already been learning "Teinei-go"! A few examples are:

- Sentences ending with "desu" (です), "masu" (ます), and "gozaimasu" (ございます)

- Words starting with the "o" (お) or "go" (ご) prefix

In the Chapter 2, when we learned the sentences structure of " – wa – desu", we already started to use "Teineigo". When we learned the greetings "ohayo gozaimsu" (おはようございます) and "arigato gozaimasu" (ありがとうございます) those are "Teineigo" as well. As mentioned, you can just greet " ohayo" (おはよう) or "arigato" (ありがとう) in casual situations.

When it comes to adding the "o" or "go" prefix in front of the noun, there is a tricky rule that determines whether either "o" or "go" is added. Not all the nouns can be prefixed with "o", and not all nouns can be prefixed with "go". The rules for this concept have many exceptions. It is best to learn each, one by one, as we go through the lessons. We'll take a look at some now:

Ryōri (りょうり) ⇨ **O**ryori (おりょうり)

Tanbōbi (たんじょうび) ⇨ **O**tanjōbi (おたんじょうび)

Yoyaku (よやく) ⇨ **Go**yoyaku (ごよやく)

Namae (なまえ) ⇨ **O**namae (おなまえ) = name

Shigoto (しごと) ⇨ **O**shigoto (おしごと) = job

When talking about your own name or your own job, you would use the form "namae"(なまえ) or "shigoto"(しごと). However, when mentioning someone else's name or job, you would use the forms of "onamae" (おなまえ) and "oshigoto" (おしごと). Perhaps you are starting to understand when "polite forms" should be used?

Something interesting in the Japanese language is that the words to refer to one's own family and another's family are *different*. As you will see below, when speaking of a third party family member, you will *always* include not only the prefix of "o", but also the suffix of "san".

English	Your Family member	Third Party family member
father	chichi (ちち/ 父)	otōsan (お父さん)
mother	haha (はは / 母)	okāsan (お母さん)

older sister	ane (あね / 姉)	onīsan (お兄さん)
older brother	ani (あに / 兄)	onēsan (お姉さん)
younger sister	imōto (いもうと / 妹	imōto san (妹さん)
younger brother	otōto (おとうと / 弟)	otōtos san (弟さん)

6.3 Avoiding the repetition

In Japanese sentences, once a topic has been mentioned, it is rare to be mentioned repeatedly. There is a tendency to omit any words which can be understood mutually. It is easy to overlook the omission of subjects and other words which would normally be included in English. Although you will be grammatically correct without the omission, as you advance your practice, you will find that refusing to omit certain words may make you sound awkward in your speeches.

Let's look at a simple example. Imagine you are meeting someone for the first time, and you would like to ask for their name. You would say,

"ONAMAE WA?"

おなまえ は？

Meaning: What is your name?

If this is literally translated to English, it would be "name is?", which may be surprising as it sounds very direct. After a whole section explaining how we need to be respectful and change verbs to raise the importance of someone else, what makes this an acceptable way of speaking? Where's the respect in this phrase? Notice that there is the added prefix of "o" (お) before "namae" (なまえ), which is the word for "name". With this added prefix, you have already changed it to the "polite form"! Since you will *not* use this form to speak of your own name, it is already known that you are speaking of another person's name. Therefore, there is no need for any other additional words. This phrase in itself is not only acceptable, but is also in the "polite form".

Now, moving on to the response. When you find yourself on the receiving end of this question, how would you respond? If we were to translate the typical English response, it would be:

WATASHI NO NAMAE WA ___ DESU.

わたしのなまえは ＿ ＿ ＿ です。

Meaning: My name is ____.

There is no absolutely grammatical error in this response *at all*. However, we did learn that it may sound awkward when we do not omit certain words when speaking. So, instead of having to say the full response above, you can simply say,

___ DESU

___　です。

Meaning: I am ___ / My name is ___

The two responses mean the exact same thing, it is simply a matter of whether you choose to or remember to omit certain words that are not necessary to the context. The best way to learn this particular skill is probably to learn from example sentences, and not fully rely on a direct translation from your native language.

6.4 Speaking Keigo as a non-native in Japan

While natives are expected to master and properly use "Keigo", (and if they do not, they sound unprofessional, ignorant, and even rude), the same is not always the case for non-native speakers. It is fair to say that foreigners are forgiven for their misuse or mistakes. However, if you do master "Keigo", it definitely conveys your passion to the language as well as the people, which is always welcomed. That being said, "Keigo" is a very important part of Japanese culture, so learning this skill would be beneficial to your connection to the culture as well as to the language.

6.5 Uchi to Soto - Uchi and Soto

Oftentimes, when we think about showing respect to others, we think of the social hierarchy. However, it is not only about showing respect to the elderly or the people with higher status. In Japanese culture, there is a very deep and fundamental concept that permeates everything, including language: it is the concept of "UCHI to SOTO". "UCHI" means "inside" or "inside house" and "SOTO" means " outside". There is always a recognition of "inside" or "outside" when speaking.

Consider a business setting. When calling your senior or your boss, you would refer to them personally as "Yamada-san", with the suffix "San". However, when you are meeting with an individual from a *different* company, you would refer to your boss as "Yamada", without the suffix. And although it may seem rude, it is due to the concept of "UCHI to SOTO" that this is acceptable. When meeting this individual from a different setting, the "SOTO" would be this individual as he is 'outside' of your space, while your boss would be your "UCHI" since you are from the same company. Therefore, you are to humble yourself – this would include your boss as well – towards the outsider. These social concepts are applied almost unconsciously for Japanese people, but it may take a bit of effort to learn this as a non-native.

✦ Quick Review ✦

☆ Japanese Honorifics can be divided into 3 groups:

<u>Respectful form</u> that is used to refer to someone's action,

<u>Humble form</u> that is to be used to refer to your own action.

Lastly with <u>polite form</u>, we can add politeness to your language.

☆ It is common to omit words that act as a repetition

☆ An important concept that underlies honorifics is "UCHI to SOTO"

☑Check list #11

Can you change these phrases to polite form / teinei-go? And check the meaning.

☐ "Arigatō"

☐ "Namae"

☐ "Shigoto"

☐ "Ryōri"

☐ "Tanjōbi"

☐ "Yoyaku"

Nihongo Trivia

NOW let's move on to a "FUN FACT" about Japanese names

In Japanese, the order of stating names is different from English.

Our name order is (Surname) + (Given name), while in English, the given name comes first, and then the surname / family name. Though calling someone by their given name is quite normal in English, it may sound too intimate, or even rude to do so in Japanese. It is a good idea to avoid calling someone by their given name when meeting them for the first time. Whether you call someone by their given name or surname, it is polite to add "san" (さん) after their name.

- "san" (さん)

"San" can be added after both male and female names, and works functionally like Mr./ Ms/ Miss/ Mrs. It can also be attached to the names of occupations and titles. For example, SAKANAYA (さかなや) means fishmonger and we call them "Sakanaya-san" (さかなや さん). Shichō means "Mayor" and we can call him / her Shichō-san (しちょう さん). Bengoshi means lawyer, therefore "Bengoshi-san" (べんごし さん) can be used as well, and so on.

- "Kun" (くん)

We use "kun"(くん) to address a person who is younger than you – specifically, a younger boy. A male might address a female by "kun," usually in schools or companies. But it is *not* used between women or when addressing someone superior to you.

- "Chan" (ちゃん)

Similarly, "chan" (ちゃん) can be attached to children's names when you call them by their given names. "Chan" is used for girls, young children, babies, close friends, and grandparents, and even for cute animals. It is used to show affection or closeness, so you should refrain from using this when addressing someone you have met for the first time.

CHAPTER 7:

Verb Sentences / All the Action Words

We have now learned how to describe nouns using noun sentences as well as adjective sentences. This means that you are developing your skill of expressing something in Japanese, but we can build upon that by learning how to express our actions with verbs. As we build upon this skill, we are getting closer to perfecting the basic skills in Japanese.

When it comes to verbs, the rule is that verbs are always placed at the end of the sentence.

In this chapter, we will be introduced to verbs in the "masu form" first. (Which is also known as "teinei-go" – as mentioned in the previous chapter.) Verbs in "masu" form can be used to describe something you are going to do in the future as well as something you do regularly or habitually. Each verb can be and would be changed into other forms, but for now we are going to perfect the usage of verbs in "masu" form. And some good news: verbs are not affected by the subject / topic – i.e. it does not matter if the subject is singular or plural, or if it is in first person or second person, etc.

In this chapter, we will learn basic verbs that are categorized into 4 groups. Within each group, we will learn the particles that are usually paired with the respective verbs.

These 4 groups are:

1. Verbs without Object
2. Verbs with Object
3. Verbs with destinations
4. Other verbs

7.1 Verbs without Objects

Verbs in this group are often used with phrases expressing time or date. Let's look at 5 verbs in this group.

Rōmaji	Hiragana	Meaning
okimasu	おきます	to get up
nemasu	ねます	to sleep
hatarakimasu	はたらきます	to work
yasumimasu	やすみます	to have a rest
owarimasu	おわります	to finish

These verbs follow the sentence structure:

```
time / days of the week      ni      (verb) ⌢masu.
    month/ date              に       ⌢ ます。
```

As you can see, the particle that is used with these particular verbs is "ni"(に). Particle "ni"(に) marks non relative times, such as time, day of the week, month and date. Particle "ni" has many other functions as well, but will be introduced later in another section of this chapter. Other useful particles to be used together with these verbs are "kara"(から) and "made" (まで).

```
(time / date ) kara  (time / date ) made
   ⌢⌢      から      ⌢⌢      まで

              (verb) ⌢masu.
                  ⌢ ます。
```

The verb "kara"(から) means "from" and "made" (まで) means "to / until". Although the examples show these particles being used together in the same sentence, they do not always have to be used together.

Example Usage

- WATASHI WA 7JI NI OKIMASU.

  o わたしは ７じに おきます。

  o Meaning: I wake up at 7.

- 12 JI KARA 12JI HAN MADE YASUMIMASU.

  o 12じ から 12じはん まで　やすみます。

  o Meaning: I rest from 12:00 to 12:30.

- GETSUYŌBI KARA HATARAKIMASU.

  o げつようび から はたらきます。

  o Meaning: I (will) work from Monday.

- 5JI HAN MADE HATARAKIMASU.

  o ごじ はん まで はたらきます。

  o Meaning: I (will) work until 5:30.

Exercise 5

Using the verbs listed above, create the following sentences:

1. "I go to bed at 11pm."

2. "What time do you usually go to bed?"

3. "I work from 9 to 5:30."

4. "Anna works from Monday to Friday."

7.2 Verbs with Objects

In this section we are covering the verbs which require an object to form a sentence. This first table will provide examples of these verbs, and the table just below will provide examples of objects.

Rōmaji	Hiragana	Meaning
tabemasu	たべます	to eat
nomimasu	のみます	to drink
mimasu	みます	to see / to look at
kikimasu	ききます	to listen
kakimasu	かきます	to write
kaimasu	かいます	to buy
yomimasu	よみます	to read
shimasu	します	to do

Rōmaji	Hiragana / Katakana	Meaning
kudamono	くだもの	fruits
mizu	みず	water
eiga	えいが	movie
ongaku	おんがく	music
tegami	てがみ	letter
kaban	かばん	bag
zasshi	ざっし	magazine
shigoto	しごと	job / work

Words for Objects the sentence structure for Verbs with Objects is:

> Object   o   verb ⌢masu.
>
> (object)   を   ⌢ ます。

Using the vocabularies from the tables, we are forming verb sentences with objects.

Example Usage

- Gohan* o tabemasu.

    o ごはん を たべます

    o Meaning: Eat meals / eat rice

- Mizu o nimimasu.

    o みず を のみます

    o Meaning: Drink water

- Eiga o yomimasu.

    o えいが を みます

    o Meaning: Watch a movie

- Ongaku o kikimasu.

    o おんがく を ききます

    o Meaning: Listen to the music

- Tegami o kakimasu.

    o てがみ を かきます

    o Meaning: Write a letter

- Kaban o kaimasu.

- o かばん を かいます

  - o Meaning: Buy a bag

- Zasshi o yomimasu.

  - o ざっし を よみます

  - o Meaning: Read a magazine

- Shigoto o shimasu.

  - o しごと を します

  - o Meaning: Do work

*The word "gohan"(ごはん) can be translated as "meal" as well as "rice". Commonly joined with words like "asa"(あさ) which means "morning","hiru"(ひる) which means "noon or daytime", "ban/yoru" (ばん / よる) which means "evening or night". The word "asa gohan" (あさごはん) means "breakfast", "hirugohan" (ひるごはん) means "lunch", and "bangohan or yorugohan" (ばんごはん/ よるごはん) means "dinner".

7.3 Verbs with destination

These are the three verbs that make up this group.

Rōmaji	Hiragana	Meaning
ikimasu	いきます	to go
kimasu	きます	to come
kaerimasu	かえります	to go back

When using the verbs with destination, the particle that is used to mark the destination is either "ni" or "e". Here is what the sentence structure looks like:

(destination)   e/ ni   verb 〜masu.

へ/ に   〜 ます。

A verb to take note of in this group is "kaerimasu"(かえります). "Kaerimasu"(かえります) means "to return to where you belong to e.g. your home / country", and so it would be used when speaking of returning to a place you consider 'home'. For example, you would not say,

IE NI IKIMASU

いえ に いきます

Instead, you would say,

IE NI KAERIMASU

いえ に かえります

Meaning: I am going home.

This is because your home is your place of belonging. You would only use "ikimasu" (いきます), if you are going to somebody else's house – since that would *not* be your place. So when speaking of going to a friend's house, you would say,

TOMODACHI NO IE NI IKIMASU.

ともだち の いえ に いきます

Meaning: I am going to my friend's home.

It is important to know how and when to use these verbs, as they can alter the meaning of sentences.

Example Usage

- Tokyo ni/ e ikimasu.

    ○ とうきょう に/ へ いきます。

    ○ Meaning:" I go to Tokyo

- Koko ni/ e kimasu.

- o ここ に/へ きます。

  - o Meaning: I (will) come here.

- Uchi ni/ e kaerimasu.

  - o うち に/へ かえります。

  - o Meaning: I (will) go home.

Another particle that is used with these verbs is the particle "de" (で). This is used when there is a method of transport included in the sentence. Let's look at some words for transportation, and then begin creating more complex sentences.

Words for Transportation

Rōmaji	Hiragana / Katakana	Meaning
densha	でんしゃ	train
chikatetsu	ちかてつ	subway
basu	バス	bus
takushī	タクシー	taxi
kuruma	くるま	car / automobile
jitensha	じてんしゃ	bicycle
hikōki	ひこうき	airplane
fune	ふね	ship /

Now that we've seen both the verbs with destination as well as words for transportation, we can create sentences using this sentence structure:

(means)   de   verb 〜masu.
で   〜 ます。

Example Usage:

- Kuruma de gakkō ni ikimasu.

  ○ くるま で がっこう に いきます

  ○ Meaning: I go to school by car.

- Jitensha de kaerimasu.

  ○ じてんしゃ で かえります

  ○ Meaning: I go home by bicycle.

Exercise 6

Choose the appropriate particle for the sentences.

1. Hiragana {o / wa } kakimasu.

2. Tokyo { o/ ni } ikimau.

3. Nanji { ni / mo } kaerimasu ka?

4. 8 ji { wa / kara } 9 ji { made / o } yasumimasu.

5. Eiga { ga / ni } suki desu ka?

7.4 Other Verbs

The verbs "aimasu"(あいます) and "hanashimasu" (はなします) are special verbs, as they mean different things when placed with different particles. The particles we will be speaking of are "to" (と) and "ni" (に).

Firstly, "aimasu"(あいます) means "to meet" and "hanashimasu" (はなします) means "to speak, to talk". The meaning of the word *itself* does not suddenly change, so do not worry about that. However, when placed with either "to"(と) or "ni"(に), they depict different scenarios. It is best to understand these concepts through examples. We will look at the meaning of sentences when placed with each of the mentioned particles.

"Aimasu' = to meet

⌒to aimasu (と あいます)

Tomodachi to aimasu. "I am going to **meet with** my friend."

⌒ni aimasu- (に あいます)

Tomodachi ni aimasu. "I am going to **see** my friend."

"Hanashimasu" = to speak / to talk

⌒ to hanashimasu (と はなします)

- Sensei to hanashimasu. "I am going to talk **with** my teacher."

⌒ ni hanashimasu (に はなします)

- Sensei ni hanashimasu. "I am going to talk **to** my teacher."

Although it may not seem significant, it is important to know the difference between the usage of the two. The particle "to"(と) can be understood as meaning "with", while the particle "ni"(に) can be understood as meaning "to"(と). Consequently, when you use "to"(と) as the particle, it depicts the scenario of doing an activity *with* someone. And if you use the "ni"(に) particle, it depicts the scenario of doing an activity *to* someone.

Do you remember the verb "shimasu"(します)? Yes, it is one of the most used verbs. We will look at the phrase, "to call", which can be written as "denwa shimasu" (でんわします) or "denwa o shimasu"(でんわ を します). "Denwa" means "phone", hence the verb means "to make a phone call". Let's see this phrase in a sentence.

〰 to denwa shimasu (と でんわします)

-Tomodachi to denwa shimasu. "I will talk **with** my friend on / over the phone."

〰 ni denwa shimasu (に でんわします)

-Tomodachi ni denwa shimasu. "I will make a phone call **to** my friend."

✦ Quick explanation ✦

☆ "Denwa shimasu" VS "denwa o shimasu"(でんわ を します)

Both mean the same, but are just slightly different ways of speaking. "Denwa shimasu" is considered to be *one verb*. "Denwa o shimasu" is an *object* (denwa) and *verb* (shimasu). This rule applies to all the following pairs as well:

☆ "benkyō o shimasu" VS "benkyō shimasu"

☆ "Kaimono o shimasu" VS "kaimono shimasu"

☆ "shigoto o shimasu" VS "shigoto shimasu"

☆ "ryoko o shimasu" VS "ryoko shimasu"

☆ "Sanpo o shimasu" VS "sanpo shimasu"

Finally we are going to look at another particle which is often used in verb sentences.

Particle "de" (で) is used to mark the place where action occurs.

(place/ location) de	verb 〜masu.
で	〜 ます。

Words for places / location

Rōmaji	Hiragana / Katakana	Meaning
hoteru	ホテル	hotel
kōen	こうえん	park
ginkō	ぎんこう	bank
toshokan	としょかん	library
kōban	こうばん	police box
kūkō	くうこう	airport
konbini	コンビニ	convenience store

Example Usage

- Gakkō de nihongo o benkyō shimasu.

  o がっこう で にほんご を べんきょう　します。

  o Meaning: I study Japanese at school

- Kaisha de hiru gohan o tabemasu.

  o かいしゃ で ひるごはん を たべます。

- o Meaning: I eat my lunch in the office.

- Sūpā de kaimono o shimasu.

    - o スーパーで かいもの を します。

    - o Meaning: I shop at the supermarket.

☑Check list #12

Can you say these phrases in Japanese?

☐ Go shopping

☐ See / Meet family

☐ Go by subway

☐ Read books

☐ Drink coffee

☐ Talk with friends

Exercise 7

Imagine this is your schedule for the day. Can you describe what you will be doing at the written times?

```
6:00    get up

6:30    do yoga

7:00    have a breakfast

9:00    go to the office

9:00 to 12:00  work

12:30  meet a friend

5:00    go back home by bus
```

```
6:00 to 7:00 study Japanese

8:00    have a dinner

9:00 to 10:00    read a book

11:00  go to bed
```

7.5 Negative form / Past tense of Verb Sentences

By simply changing the "masu" as followed, you can express the negative form, past tense, as well as negative past sentences. This formula is one of the most welcomed rules in Japanese grammar, as it is very easy to remember!

masu(present)   masen (present negative)
〜ます   〜ません

mashita (past)   masendeshita (past negative)
〜ました   〜ませんでした

Example Usage

Using the time related vocabularies that we learned in the chapter 4, we can construct the sentences such as:

- Watashi wa niku o tabemasen.

    o わたしは にくをたべません。

    o Meaning: I do not eat meat

- Kinō hon o kaimashita.

    o きのう ほんを かいました。

o Meaning:"I bought a book yesterday."

If you are interested in adding more details to your sentences, here are some words to express frequency. They are very helpful and are a simple way to create more depth to your sentences!

Words for frequency

Rōmaji	Hiragana	Meaning
mainichi	まいにち	everyday
maiasa	まいあさ	every morning
maiban	まいばん	every night
yoku	よく	often
tokidoki	ときどき	sometimes
amari	あまり	no so often
zenzen	ぜんぜん	not at all

*Amari (あまり) Zenzen (ぜんぜん) should always be used in negative sentences

Example Usage

- Otōto wa amari benkyō shimasen.

  o おとうと は あまり べんきょうしません。

  o Meaning: My brother doesn't study often.

- Tokidoki wain o nomimasu.

  o ときどき ワイン を のみます。

  o Meaning: Sometimes (I) drink wine.

Exercise 8

Change the ending of the sentence to the appropriate form.

1. Senshū ryokō ni (ikimasu) ⇨ ....

2. Sakana o amari (tabemasu) ⇨ ....

3. Kinō tomodachi wa (kimasu) ⇨ ....*did not come

4. Kūkō ni zenzen (ikimasu) ⇨ ....

5. Hirugohan wa (tabemasu) ⇨ .... * did not eat

Nihongo Trivia

Do you know Japanese internet slang?　日本語のスラング

If you are someone engaged with Japanese social media, or maybe have a Japanese friend that you message, you may have encountered a social media post or message from someone with the letter "w". It could be part of a whole paragraph, or simply on its own. Yes, just "w". A bit strange if you have never been exposed to it. But let's find out what it means, because yes, it does have a meaning!

"W" is the equivalent to "lol" in English text slang. You may be thinking, yes, because "lol" stands for "laughing out loud"! What would "w" stand for?

The "W" comes from the verb "waraimasu / warau" which means " to laugh". It can be just "W", or some would write it as "ww" or "www". You may also see just one kanji character "笑", as this is the character for laugh, "warai" "笑い"(わらい). In the case of the kanji, it is usually written in parenthesis, like (笑).

This is something you can use when you begin engaging in message with your Japanese friends. It may feel strange typing this, but do not worry, you will be well understood!

CHAPTER 8:

Various expressions:

Existence, Past tense of Adjectives, Comparison and Desire

8.1 Existence / Arimasu or Imasu

To express existence in Japanese, which is equivalent to "there is" and "there are" in English, we use verbs "arimasu" (あります) or "imasu" (います).

In this chapter we will learn the difference between these two verbs, as well as useful vocabulary to specify the position of the existence of any people or objects.

When the subject or topic of the sentence is an *inanimate* thing, we use "arimasu". While "imasu" is used when the subject or topic is something *animate*. You may be tempted to decide whether the subject/topic is animate or inanimate by knowing whether it is living or nonliving. However, that is not the case here. Inanimate subjects include things that may be alive, but cannot move by itself or by its own will.

Have a think about plants. Plants are living things but they cannot move by themselves. Therefore, by this definition, we would label plants as inanimate, and use "arimasu" to express their existence. If we speak of fish swimming in the ocean? Of course, "imasu" is applied. How about if there is fish being packed and waiting to be sold in a market? Since they cannot move by themselves, we would use "arimasu."

As you can see, "arimasu" and "imasu" are not as easily used as the English phrases "there is" or "there are". These English phrases can be used whether or not the subject or topic is animate. Let's look at some sentences to really grasp this concept:

Example Usage

- Koko ni hon ga arimasu.

o ここに ほん が あります。

o Meaning: There is a book here.

● Amerika ni kazoku ga imasu.

o アメリカ に かぞく が います

o Meaning: I have a family in America."

Have the example sentences helped with your understanding? You may have noticed the use of particle "に" (ni) in these sentences. This is the basic sentence structure you can use when creating sentences with ARIMASU and IMASU.

> (place) ni (thing) ga arimasu
> 〜 に 〜 が あります
>
> OR
>
> (place) ni (people/ animal) ga imasu
> 〜 に 〜 が います

Another important point that we have to pay attention to is the particle "ni"(に) to mark the place/ location of existence.

8.2 Positioning words

When you wish to convey the position of an object, you would join a positioning word to a noun, using the particle "の" (no). This creates the following sentence pattern:

> (reference noun) +no+ position word
> 〜 の 〜

The table below summarizes some positioning words.

Rōmaji	Rōmaji	Meaning
ue	うえ	on, above
shita	した	under, below
migi	みぎ	right side
hidari	ひだり	left side
naka	なか	inside
soto	そと	outside
mae	まえ	In front
ushiro	うしろ	behind
yoko	よこ	beside
tonari	となり	next to
mukai	むかい	opposite of
chikaku	ちかく	nearby

Example Usage:

- Tsukue no ue
  - つくえ の うえ
  - Meaning: On top of the table
- Tsukue no shita
  - つくえ の した
  - Meaning: Under the table

- Isu no migi

  - いす の みぎ

  - Meaning: The right side of the chair

- Isu no hidari

  - いす の ひだり

  - Meaning: The left side of the chair

- Hako no naka

  - はこ の なか

  - Meaning: Inside the box

- Hako no soto

  - はこ の そと

  - Meaning: Outside the box

- Kodomo no mae

  - こども の まえ

  - Meaning: In front of the children

- Kodomo no ushiro

  - こども の うしろ

  - Meaning: Behind the children

- Neko no tonari

  - ねこ の となり

  - Meaning: Next to the cat

- Konbini no mukai

  - コンビニ の むかい

  - Meaning: Opposite of the convenient store

- Ie no chikaku / soba

    o いえ の ちかく/ そば

    o Meaning: Close to the house

When you need to ask who or what exists in the place.

We can use "dare" (だれ) for people, and "nani" (なに) for animals and things.

The below is the example format.

> (place) ni dare ga imasu ka
>
> (place) に だれ が います か
>
> Meaning: Who is in/ at the place?
> (existence of people)
>
> (place) ni nani ga imasu ka
>
> (place) に なに が います か
>
> meaning: What is in/ at the place?
> (existence of animal)
>
> (place) ni nani ga arimasu ka
>
> (place) に なに が あります か
>
> meaning: What is in/ at the place?
> (existence of thing)

Example Usage

- Heya ni dare ga imasu ka?

    o へや に だれが います か

    o Meaning: Who is in the room?

- Dabide san ga imasu

- o ダビデ が います

    - o Meaning: Davide is in the room.

- Isu no shita ni nani ga imasu ka?

    - o いす の した に なに が いますか

    - o Meaning: What is under the chair?

- Neko ga imasu

    - o ねこ がいます

    - o Meaning: There is a cat.

- Hako no naka ni nani ga arimasu ka

    - o はこ の なか に なに が ありますか

    - o Meaning: What is there in the box?

- Purezento ga arimasu

    - o プレゼント が あります

    - o Meaning: There is a present in it.

☑Check list ☐ #13

Can you say these greeting phrases in Japanese?

☐ "Right side of the bag"

☐ "Near the house"

☐ "Outside of the station"

☐ "Under the tree"

☐ "In front of me"

8.3 Counters

When describing the number of things or people in English, we simply state the number and the objects, for example, "three people" or "four cats".

However, in Japanese, we need to use something called 'counters' for stating the number of the objects. These 'counter' words actually change depending on what object you are referring to. There are quite a number of counters to be studied, but they will all be summarized in the table below.

Counter Words:

Rōmaji	hiragana/ kanji	Describes:
hon	ほん / 本	long and thin objects e.g. a pen, a umbrella
dai	だい / 台	large objects (or machinery) e.g.a car, a bicycle
mai	まい / 枚	thin and flat objects e.g. paper, T-shirt
ko	こ / 個	general counting / Small objects e.g. candy or orange
nin	にん / 人	people
hiki/ biki	ひき・びき / 匹	animals
hai	はい / 杯	glasses or cup of liquid
satsu	さつ / 冊	books or magazines
kai	かい / 階	floors of the building
kai	かい / 回	frequency of something happens ,"times" in English

Let's look at some simple examples of stating the number of objects using the respective counters. The phrase with the counter words normally comes before the verb as highlighted below.

Example Usage

- Pen ga gohon arimasu.

  o ペン が ごほん あります。

  o Meaning: There are five pens.

- Neko ga nihiki imasu.

  o ねこ が にひき います。

  o Meaning: There are two cats.

Similar to how there are exceptions in pronunciation when it comes to dates and time in minutes, there are also such exceptions here. These exceptions are of the counter word 'hon' (ほん / 本). Depending on the number that is being expressed, the pronunciation also changes:

ippon	いっぽん
nihon	にほん
sanbon	さんぼん
yonhon	よんほん
gohon	ごほん
roppon	ろっぽん
nanahon	ななほん
happon	はっぽん
kyūhon	きゅうほん
juppon	じゅっぽん

We need to pay attention as well to the counter word "nin" (にん / 人) – when we are counting the number of people. However, it is a bit less complicated than "hon" because there are only two changes. When counting one person and two people, you would say:

- Hitori　ひとり　one person

- Futari　ふたり　two people

These are the only two changes to be aware of! Once you count three people and more, you would simply revert to the number + "nin" structure. For example,

- San nin　さんにん　three people

- Yonin　よにん　four people

Luckily, there is a generic counter that can be used in most cases, but only for inanimate/ non living objects.

hitotsu	ひとつ
futatsu	ふたつ
mittsu	みっつ
yottsu	よっつ
itsutsu	いつつ
muttsu	むっつ
nanatsu	ななつ
yattsu	やっつ
kokonotsu	ここのつ
tō	とう

Example Usage

- Mikan ga mittsu arimasu

  - みかん が みっつ あります

OR

- Mikan ga sanko arimasu

  - みかん が さんこ あります

These sentences are interchangeable and both mean: "There are three oranges".

There are also instances where you would not mention an exact number, but rather mention something such as, " a lot" or " a little bit". In these cases, you can use the words:

Rōmaji	Hiragana	meaning:
takusan	たくさん	a lot, lots of, many
sukoshi	すこし	a little bit, few, small amount

8.4 Past tense of Adjectives

To form the past tense of adjective sentences, our grouping of i-adjectives and na-adjectives becomes important. To make the past tense form of i-adjectives, you do so simply by changing "i" to "katta". For past negative forms for i-adjectives, you can change "i" to "kunakatta".

〜い ⇨ 〜かった (past tense) です

〜 i 　　　〜katta desu

⇨ 〜くなかった (past negative) です

〜kunakatta desu

If we want to change the i-adjective of "yoi" to it's past tense, it would be:

YOI ⇨ YOKATTA DESU

よい ⇨ よかった です

Meaning: "It was nice"

As mentioned in Chapter 3, "yoi" and "ii", both mean "good". When you wish to change it to past tense, you can only use "yoi".

Taking again the example of "yoi", if we wish to change it to past tense in negative for, it would be:

YOI ⇨ YOKUNAKATTA DESU

よい ⇨ よくなかった です

Meaning: It was not good.

We can look at other i-adjective examples:

(Positive form)

ATSUI ⇨ ATSUKATTA DESU

あつい ⇨ あつかった です

Meaning: It was hot

—

(Negative form)

ATSUI ⇨ ATSUKU NAKATTA DESU

あつい ⇨ あつくなかった です

Meaning: "It was not hot"

—

To form the past tense of na-adjectives, you would remove the "na", and you add "deshita" at the end of the adjective. For instance, the na-adjective "Kirei na", will be changed to "kirei", and then add the "deshita" to create "kirei deshita". The negative form requires the addition of "dewa arimasen deshita", which will create the full phrase that is "kirei dewa arimasen deshita"

〜です ⇨ 〜でした (past tense)

〜 desu 〜deshita

⇨ 〜ではありませんでした (past negative)

〜dewa arimasen deshita

8.5 Expressions of comparison

Comparing two options

The Japanese language does not include comparative forms of adjectives, such as ~er or ~est in English. We express comparison by using either the phrase "~no hō ga" (のほうが), or the word, "yori" (より). The phrase "~no hō ga" is similar to the English use of "more" or "better", while "yori" is similar to the English use of "than".

Comparing Two :

（A） のほうが （B） より 〜〜です

（A） no hō ga （B） yori 〜〜 desu

For example, to say " China is bigger than Japan", you would say:

Chūgoku wa nihon yori ōkii desu.

ちゅうごく は にほん より おおきい です。

The word "yori" (より) was used for comparison in this sentence. China is the topic, which is why it begins the sentence and has the particle "wa" (は). This sentence structure is a direct translation to "China is bigger than Japan.". You may also use the phrase "no hō ga" (のほうが) and "yori" (より) to express the same content with a slight difference.

Chūgoku no ho ga ōkii.

ちゅうごく のほう が おおきい です。

Chūgoku no ho ga nihon yori ōkii.

ちゅうごく の ほうが にほん より おおきい です。

As you can see, the first sentence simply means, "China is bigger", while the second is more detailed in saying "China is bigger than Japan". From this you may understand that the phrase "no hō ga" (のほうが) already expresses the idea that there has been a selection made. "Chugoku no ho ga ōkii" can only really be said if you are being asked a question such as "Which is bigger, China or japan?"(chūgoku to nihon to dochira ga ōkii desu ka?). Then you could answer by just saying that "China is bigger". So, if you are answering a question where you have been given two options, you can use the first sentence. If you are making a statement that stands on its own, then you would use the second statement. Hopefully the difference between the two are clear.

Comparing three or more options

Now we are going to look at the phrase that expresses "the most" by using "ichiban" (いちばん).

The literal translation of "ichiban" is "number one", but it also means "the most' or " the best". When comparing three or more things, we can use "ichiban" (いちばん) followed by the adjective of choice.

Let's start with a phrase to express "most interesting". This would be,

Ichiban omoshiroi desu

いちばん おもしろい です

Or if you would like to say, "the prettiest", it would be:

Ichiban kirei desu

いちばん きれい です

But of course, we want to add more details. When speaking of multiple things / comparing multiple things, we use the particle "de" to mark the range of topics. This is the equivalent to 'among' in English. For example,

Kono naka de kore ga ichiban suki desu.

このなかで これ が いちばん すき です。

Meaning: Among these, I like this best.

Comparing Three or more :

〜で　〜が　いちばん〜〜です

〜de　〜ga　ichiban〜〜 desu

If we want to be more specific, we can say something like,

Nihon de fujisan ga ichiban takai desu.

にほん　で　ふじさん　が　いちばん　たかい　です。

OR

Fujisan wa nihon de ichiban takai desu.

ふじさん　は　にほん　で　いちばん　たかい　です。

Both sentences mean: "Mt Fuji is the highest in Japan".

We can connect back to our knowledge of wh- words – i.e. what or who – to create our very own questions. We'll take a look at sentences to ask "___ do you like best?", and simply change the interrogative in the beginning of the sentence.

Dore ga ichiban suki desuka?

どれ が いちばん すき です か。

Meaning: Which do you like best?

Dare ga ichiban suki desuka?

だれ が いちばん すき ですか。

Meaning: Who do you like best?

Do ko ga ichiban suki desuka?

どこ が いちばん すき ですか。

Meaning: Where do you like best?

——

☑Check list ☐ #14

Can you say these greeting phrases in Japanese?

☐ "It was hot today. Today was hot."

☐ "I bought 3 eggs."

☐ "Who is most kind in your family?"

☐ "The movie was not interesting."

☐ "I like summer better than winter." * summer = natsu / winter = fuyu

8.6 Expressing your desire

When wanting to express our desires in Japanese, we can use either the words, "〜 tai desu" (〜たいです) or "〜 hoshii desu" (ほしい です).

"〜 tai" is used to express your desire to do something, and thus connects to a verb.

"〜 hoshii" is attached to a noun that you desire to have.

> ~ tai desu
> たい ⇨ verb + ~~ます~~たい　です
>
>
> ~ hoshii desu
> ほしい ⇨ noun + が　ほしい　です

To use "tai desu" (〜たいです), you would take the verb in "masu form", omit the "masu"(ます), and attach "tai"(たい) instead.

To use "hoshii desu"(ほしい です), you mark the object you desire to have with the particle "ga"(が), followed by the phrase, "hoshii"(ほしい) or "hoshii desu"(ほしい です).

Example Usage

- Konban tomodachi to wain wo nomitai desu.

  o こんばん ともだちと ワインを のみたい です。

  o Meaning: I want to drink wine with my friends tonight.

- Atarashii kaban wo kaitai desu.

  o あたらしい かばん を かいたい です。

  o Meaning: I want to buy a new bag.

- Atarashii kaban ga hosshii desu.

- あたらしい かばん が ほしい です。

- Meaning: I want a new bag.

We can apply the same rule to both "tai' and "hoshii" when changing their forms to its negative or past tense. You may notice that those rules are the same as "i-adjectives"!

8.7 The Third party's desire

When describing a third person's desire, we do not use "tai" (たい) or "hoshii" (ほしい). Instead of "tai" (たい), we need to use "tagatte imasu"(たがっています), and "hoshii" (ほしい) should replaced by "hoshigatte imasu"(ほしがっています). The object marker "ga" (が) has to be replaced by particle "o" (を).

The reason why we need to use different phrases to express the third party's desire is the Japanese mentality that we do not decide for others. In this case, you do not define someone else's desire. The third person's desire form is almost as if we are speaking on the behalf of others. Therefore, we cannot use the same phrases we use to describe our *own* desires to describe the desires of others.

For third person's desire

たい　⇨　　たがって　います

verb + ~~ます~~ tagatte imasu

ほしい　⇨　　〜を　ほしがって　います

noun + o hoshigatte imasu

Example Usage

- Imōto wa/ ga* ryokō ni ikitagatte imasu

  o いもうと は/が りょこう に いきたがって います。

  o Meaning: My sister wants to go for a trip.

- Kodomo wa/ ga *omocha wo hoshigatte imasu.

  o こども は/が おもちゃ を ほしがって います。 *omocha = a toy

  o Meaning: My / The kid wants a toy

*Both "wa" and "ga" can be used to mark the topic/ subject in this sentence pattern.

☑Check list ☐ #15

Can you say these greeting phrases in Japanese?

☐ I want to go to Hokkaidō next year.

☐ My sister wants to home early.

☐ My friend wants a new bag.

Nihongo Trivia

Ohitori- sama (おひとり さま) Culture

We have learned the word "hitori" in Chapter 8.3, "hitori"(ひとり) means "one person". "Ohitori-sama" (おひとり さま) is the result of adding the honorific "o"

(お) of teinei-go in front, and even adding a honorific suffix of 'sama' (さま) at the end.

This word "Ohitori sama" (おひとり さま) was proposed in the late '90s by a female journalist.

The original meaning was to describe how a woman could freely decide how to live alone as an independent person – i.e. having personal hobbies she enjoys or traveling alone. As time has passed, the meaning of this word has also evolved, and now refers mainly to a person who goes to a store alone, or does an activity by oneself – no longer limited to females.

Nowadays, what is known as "Ohitori sama" (おひとり さま) services are gaining popularity. There are many services that are opening up for people opting for activities to do alone.

There are activities that are usually done with a group or at least another person, namely Karaoke (カラオケ) or BBQ / "yakiniku" (やきにく). However, such places are accommodating to "ohitori sama" (おひとり さま), by providing spaces such as "hitori karaoke" (ひとりカラオケ), where one can enjoy a Karaoke (カラオケ) night to his/herself!

As a result of this "ohitori sama" (おひとり さま) culture, it is getting more socially acceptable to enter restaurants alone as well. In Japan, it was more likely to enter a "yakiniku" (やきにく) restaurant, or Korean BBQ restaurant, with friends or family. Now, these restaurants are providing "Hitori yakiniku"(ひとり やきにく) services for those who choose a night of "yakiniku" (やきにく)by themselves!

How does the "Ohitoi-sama" (おひとり さま) culture sound to you? One may be hesitant to try a night of Karaoke (カラオケ) or "yakiniku" (やきにく) by themselves, but maybe it will turn out to be more enjoyable than expected!

CHAPTER 9:

Keep the Conversation going!

Isn't it nice that you can initiate the conversation and invite someone to do something together? Now we are starting with an expression of invitation. In this chapter we will master invitation expressions, as well as useful expressions to keep your conversation going. All the while building your communication skills as well as deepening your understanding of Japanese culture.

9.1 Invitation expression offering and responding

Grammatically it is very simple to make phrases of invitations as well as accept invitations in Japanese. Changing the verb "masu" to "masenka" (ません か) implies the meaning of invitation or suggestion to do something together. When we change "masu" to "mashō" (ましょう) it means "let's do".

For responding to those invitations, we can use some expressions like "ii desu ne" (いいですね) which means "that's sounds good" or "sō shimasho" (そう しましょう) which means " let's do so".

Words such as "issho ni" (いっしょに) which means "together" are very useful when you are inviting someone.

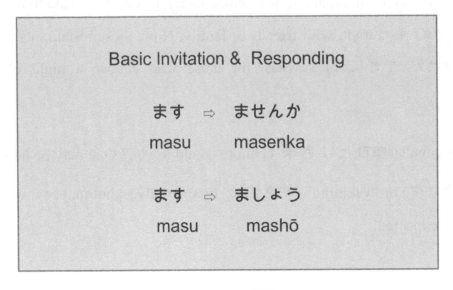

Basic Invitation & Responding

ます ⇨ ませんか
masu　　masenka

ます ⇨ ましょう
masu　　mashō

Example Usage

- Ashita konsāto ni ikimasu. Issho ni konsāto ni ikimasen ka?

  ○ あした コンサート に いきます。いっしょ に コンサート に いきませんか。

- Hai, ikimasho.

  ○ はい、 いきましょう。

- Eiga o mimasu. Issho ni mimasenka?

  ○ えいが を みます。　いっしょ に みませんか。

- Ii desune. Mimasho.

  ○ いい ですね。みましょう。

- Ryoko ni ikimasenka?

  ○ りょこう に いきませんか。

- Ii desune. Itsu ikimasho ka?

  ○ いい ですね。いつ いきましょう か。

- Raishu wa do desuka?

  ○ らいしゅう は どう ですか。

- Hai, so shimasho

  ○ はい、そうしましょう。

This was an example of accepting an offer. How about when you need to decline someone's offer?

Declining someone's offer

In Japanese there is a very useful word, "Chotto"(ちょっと). "Chotto" (ちょっと) means "a little" or "a bit". This word is often used to decline an offer. Japanese people do not directly say "no", but rather answer with "chotto…" (ちょっと、、、). When you begin your response with "chotto"(ちょっと), people will know that a negative answer is pending.

One common phrase is, "Chotto muzukaii"(ちょっと むずかしい), which translates to "a little difficult". This is essentially the equivalent to saying "no". Here is an example invitation and response in such circumstances:

- Ashita konsāto ni ikimasen ka?

    o あした コンサート に いきませんか。

- Ashita wa chotto…

    o あしたは ちょっと、、、

OR

- Konsāto wa chotto…

    o コンサートは ちょっと、、、

The use of "Chotto" (ちょっと) can be when you find yourself in "a situation in which it is difficult to make a clear decision of judgment". When speaking Japanese, you tend to take into account the feelings of the other person rather than directly express your own. Even with your close friends, you do not turn down others' offers bluntly. If you feel that only saying "chotto" may end up creating a cold impression, you can always add other phrases like "sore ii ne", "gomen", or "zannen" (ざんねん), which can translate as " it is pity, so pitiful."

9.2 Phrases for conversation

The Japanese language is full of interesting expressions that are useful for smooth communications with others. The use of such words and phrases can be telling of your character. Let's take a look at basic phrases you would want to be equipped with.

- Sumimasen / Sumimasen deshita (すみません /すみませんでした)

Both "sumimasen" and "sumimasen deshita" are very common phrases to use in daily conversations. Though the direct translation would be "i apologise", or "i am sorry", it can also be used to express "excuse me". You will come to realize how unique this phrase is, when you understand that this *one* phrase can actually convey a number of feelings simultaneously.

To be more accurate with the definition of "Sumimasen", it is actually a combination of the feelings, "I'm sorry" and "Thank you" at the same time. Or, it can mean only "excuse me", depending on the situation / context. Sumimasendeshita is the past tense of "sumimasen", and is used to refer to an occasion that occurred in the past. These phrases carry sincere humbleness to convey the message of apology as well as gratitude.

- Gomennasai （ごめんなさい）

"Gomennasai" means "I'm sorry", and it is used to show one's apology. This word carries the similar meaning as "sumimasen" but does not include the meaning of "thank you" or gratitude in it. Japanese people tend to use "gomennasai" for quite minor inconvenience they may have caused, or even in situations where they were not at fault for any inconvenience. You will find yourself hearing this word on a multitude of occasions when interacting with Japanese natives.

- The difference between " sumimasen" and "gomennasai"

Japanese language learners often encounter the confusion between "sumimasen" and "gomenasai", as they are about to express their apology. Both "Sumimasen" and "gomenasai" can be used when you have made a mistake or caused someone any inconvenience. For the most part, it comes down to a matter of your personal preference. Apart from the difference that was already mentioned ("Sumimasen" can be used to express the feeling of gratitude, though "gomennasai" cannot be used in such a situation) , there are a few other subtle differences that can be taken into consideration.

1. Generally, "Sumimasen" is slightly more formal than "Gomennasai"

2. In the situation where you need to apologize to someone higher than you, "Sumimasen" is more appropriate.

3. Among family members or close friends, it is more common to use "Gomennasai". You can opt for "Gomen" in more casual cases.

4. When you are speaking to someone superior or people with whom you are not so close, "Sumimasen" or even the more polite word "Moushiwake arimasen" （もうしわけ ありません) are used. "Gomennasai" (ごめんなさい) can be perceived as quite childish.

- Wakarimashita (わかりました)

The word "wakarimasu" means "to understand" or "to comprehend", and the past tense of this is "wakarimashita". To assure the speaker that the listener is following and understanding what is being told or spoken, Japanese people normally use the word "wakarimashita". Even though it is in past tense, "wakarimashita" is used to show you are following the conversation in the moment, or to show you were unaware of something until you were told it. "Wakarimasu" is used when you already knew of something before being told.

Remember to use the past tense in these situations, as replying with "wakarimasu" can sound quite rebellious, and also imply that you were already aware of that information prior.

When wanting to convey the message that you do not understand, you simply reply with the negative form, which is "wakarimasen" (わかりません)– i.e. "i do not understand".

- Mō ichido onegai shimasu (もう いちど おねがいします)

The direct translation of the phrase, "Mō ichido onegai shimasu" would be "One more time please". "Ichido" means "once", and "mō" means "more". This phrase is very useful when you are unable to catch what someone said or could not understand what has been said. It is a very polite phrase and can be used in any situation. It may sound too direct when it is translated into English, but this is not the case in Japanese. The word "Onegai shimasu" means "please" and it is a very useful word as well, and will be explained below.

- Dōzo (どうぞ)

The word "dōzo" is an expression used very frequently, in situations where the speaker is offering something to the listener. The translation would be "please", or "go ahead", in situations where you are giving your way to someone. It can also mean "Please accept this" when you are handing any item such as a gift to someone.

- Yoroshiku onegai shimasu (よろしく おねがいします)

This phrase is very important for Japanese learners as it is used when you introduce yourself to someone for the first time. It is essential in the Japanese language and you will hear it often, but once again it can be a little challenging to understand the exact meaning. There are two important situations in which you would use this phrase.

1. Meeting someone for the first time. You typically introduce yourself by stating your name and this phrase. In chapter 2 /2.6 we have learned the phrase, "hajimemashite" which translation would be "nice to meet you (for the first time). You can greet by saying both "hajimemashite" and "yoroshiku onegaishimasu".

2. When you are asking someone to help you or asking for their cooperation. For example, when asking someone to complete a task or a favor, you would mention your request and add the phrase "yoroshiku onegai shimasu."

Since we just learned the word "dōzo", we can combine "dōzo" to create an even more polite introduction for yourself. You would add "dōzo" to "yoroshiku onegaishimasu", to create the full phrase of "dōzo yoroshiku onegaishimasu", to convey a very polite first impression.

- Kudasai & Onegai shimasu (ください & おねがいします)

When you try to translate the English word "please" to Japanese, you will find the words "kudasai" or "onegai shimasu". Both "kudasai" and "onegai shimasu" can be roughly translated as "please " or "please give me", and are both used when making requests. There are some occasions where it is more appropriate to use "kudasai" than "onegai shimasu" and vice versa. In general, choosing between "kudasai" and "Onegai shimasu" depends on the social context. We are going to look at each word in more depth:

How to use "kudasai" in a sentence

"Kudasai" is derived from the verb "kudasaru" which is the humble honorific verb of "kureru"(くれる). The verb "kureru / kuremasu" (くれる /くれます) means "(someone) give me". Hence, "kudasai" is used when you need to get something from someone you are speaking to. "Kudasai" is used when requesting something that you are entitled to have. In most cases, it is used in situations with your friend, peer, or someone who is considered to be in a lower status than you.

Grammatically, you need to mark the object with "o" before the word "kudasai", such as "mizu o kudasai" (water, please) or "kore o kudasai" (give me this one , please."

How to use "onegaimshimasu" in a sentence

The phrase "onegai shimasu" comes from the word "negai" (ねがい): which means "hope" or "wish". Therefore when you say "onegai shimasu", you are humbly asking someone for a favor. The translation would be "I would like that, please." or "would you please.."

While "kudasai" is a more casual term, "onegaishimasu" is the more polite or honorific way of requesting. It is used when you need to make a direct request to a superior or someone you do not know well. Similar to "kudasai", you mark the object with "o", to create "mizu o onegai shimasu." If we compare these two sentences, the latter sentence with "onegai shimasu" has a more humble tone to it.

However, the huge difference between "kudasai" and "onegaishimasu" is that "onegai shimasu" can stand alone. You can just say "hai, onegai shimasu." (yes, please.) or "onegai shimasu.". It also can be used to request something abstract in a phrase such as "yoroshiku onegai shimasu." "yoroshiku onegai shimasu" can be translated in a number of ways, such as " I hope things goes well" or " I hope that you can treat me well" or "hoping for good relations between us" and so on. The most important thing to note in this phrase of " yoroshiku onegai shimasu" is that it is used with regards to something that will happen in the future. It is not used to mention something that already happened.

You can use "onegai shimasu" when you ask for abstract or non-tangible things, such as understanding, explanation, or cooperation. Also, it is used to request any service that you cannot fulfill by yourself, such as " Tokyo eki made onegai shimasu" when you are asking the taxi driver to go to Tokyo.

☑Check list #16

Do you know the meaning of these phrases?

☐ "Wakarimasen"

☐ "Sumimasen"

☐ "Dōzo"

☐ "Onegai shimasu"

☐ "Gomennasai"

9.3 Japanese conjunctive words

Conjunctive words are also known as sentence connectors. Two sentences or clauses are connected by conjunctive words. In English, the words "and", "or", "but", and "therefore" are important conjunctions used in daily conversations.

In this section, we are going to cover some of the most common conjunctions and learn how they are used in simple sentences.

Rōmaji	Hiragana	meaning
dakara	だから	so, therefore,consequently
sorede	それで	and, and then, so
demo	でも	however, though, even though
keredo(mo)	けれど(も)	however, though, even though, yet

soshite	そして	and, and now, then
sorekara	それから	and, after that

"Dakara" (だから) and "sorede" (それで)

These are called "resultative conjunction" which imply a natural result or consequences that follow what was stated earlier on.

Example Usage

- Mainichi heya no souji wo shimasu. Dakara heya wa itumo kireri desu.

  o まいにち へや の そうじをします。 だから へや は いつも きれい です。

- Kesa hayaku okimashita. Sorede ima totemo *nemui desu. (*nemui = sleepy)

  o けさ はやく おきました。 それで いま とても ねむい です。

"Demo"(でも) and " keredo (mo)" (けれど (も))

These are "contradictory conjunctions", which have the meaning of "but' or "even though". It is used to express the opposition which doesn't result in the previous sentence, at the same time these can be used to express something unexpected or feelings of discontent.

Example Usage

- Fujisan wa totemo kirei deshita. Demo shashin wo torimasen deshita.

  o ふじさん は とても きれい でした。 でも しゃしん を とりません でした。

  o Meaning: Mt Fuji was very beautiful. But, I didn't take a photo.

- Mainichi 7ji ni okimsu. Keredo kyo wa *osoku okimashita. (*osoku = late)

  o まいにち ７じ に おきます。 けれど きょうは おそく おきました。

  o Meaning: Everyday I wake up at 7a.m. But, today I woke up late.

"Soshite" (そして) and "sorekara" (それから)

These conjunctions are called conditional conjunctions, which is used to provide additional information or conditions to the previous sentence.

The word "soshite" (そして) is simply translated as "and" in English while "sorekara" (それから) is more focused on the timeline, and implies a chronological order. If we look at the word carefully, we notice that this word consists of two components, which is "sore" (それ) and "kara"(から).

Both of which we have already learned, that "sore" (それ) is the demonstrative noun that refers to something that is not close to the speaker. "Kara" (から) is a particle which is used to refer to where something starts – the equivalent to "from" in English. Putting these two components together, they formed the expression, "from that".

Example Usage

- Ban gohan o tsukurirmashita. Soshite kazuku to tabemashita.

  ○ ばんごはん を つくりました。 そして かぞく と たべました。

  ○ Meaning: I cooked dinner, and ate with my family.

- Okāsan ga kimashita. Sorekara otōsan mo kimashita.

  ○ おかあさん が きました。 それから おとうさん も きました。

  ○ Meaning: My mother came, and then my father came as well.

☑Check list #17

Do you know the meaning of these phrases?

☐ "Dakara"

☐ "Demo"

☐ "Soshite"

☐ "Sorekara"

Nihongo Trivia

The delightfulness of the Japanese Language

A message for you:

The Japanese language is a complex and fascinating language. Many characteristics make it distinct from other languages in the world. With this guide book, I hope you have experienced the beauty of the writing systems, found fascination in the use of honorifics, and enjoyed your journey of getting to know Japanese culture.

Language is for us to share our experiences, our thoughts, and enjoy our time spent with those we care about. After all, the most important thing is your passion towards the culture and people. An open mind will always result in a good experience with other cultures. Even if you have yet to master the basics of the language, that's not really *that* important, is it? As long as you are trying your best, and appreciating the joyful moments that come.

Your journey with this guide ends here, but I hope the knowledge that you acquired will lead you to more exciting experiences and fulfillment in your life.

Thank you.

CHAPTER 10:

Practice Practice Practice!

Learning a new language means trying to learn the grammar rules, remembering all new words that you have never been exposed to, *and* coping with the overwhelming number of exceptions, rules, etc. It may be easy to question whether or not you are actually making progress with the language, and if it is even possible to look forward to a day where none of this feels difficult anymore. Do not worry, we have all felt the same at one point or another. It is quite normal to start questioning your progress if you do not have an opportunity to check or verify that you are indeed understanding what you have learned.

But, that is what this chapter is dedicated to! You have the chance to check the knowledge and skills that you have acquired over past chapters with comprehension activities. All the passages are designed to be understood without making an effort to search the meaning of the new words or learning new grammar. Vocabulary that has yet to be introduced in previous chapters are limited in number, and is marked and explained at the bottom of the passage.

These passages are designed to cover all the grammar lessons that we have gone through. They are written in Rōmaji as well as in Hiragana, so you can easily check your hiragana proficiency.

Finally, the translations of the passages are presented for you to check whether your understanding matches with its translation.

Practice 1: Hajimemashite

Konnichiwa. Hajimemashite. Arisu desu. Igirisu kara kimashita.

Nihon no kaisha de hataraite imasu.

Mainichi isogashii desu. Demo totemo tanoshii desu.

Shumi wa ryori desu. eiga mo suki desu.

Yasumi no hi ni yoku eiga o mimasu.

Tomodachi to ikimasu.

Nihon ryori no hō ga igirisu ryori yori suki desu.

Resutoran de nihon ryori o tabemasu.

Soshite ie de sono nihon ryori o tukurimasu.

Sukoshi muzukashii desu.

Demo takusan ryori o tsukuritai desu.

* "hataraite imasu" = working

* "shumi" = hobby

はじめまして

こんにちは はじめまして

アリス です イギリス から ました。

にほん の かいしゃ で はたらいて います。

まいにち いそがしい です。 でも とても たのしいです。

しゅみ は りょうりです。えいが も すきです。

やすみ の ひに よく えいが を みます。

ともだち と いきます。

にほん りょうり の ほうが イギリスりょうりより すきです。

レストラン で にほんりょうり を たべます。

そして いえ で その にほんりょうり を つくります。

すこし むずかしい です。

でも たくさん りょうり を つくりたいです。

Meaning:

How do you do?

Hello, nice to meet you. I am Alice, and I come from England.

I am working in a Japanese company.

I am busy everyday, but I am enjoying it.

My hobby is cooking, and I like watching movies as well.

I often go to watch movies on my off days.

I go with my friends.

I like Japanese cuisine better than English cuisine.

I eat Japanese food at a restaurant, and cook the dish at home.

I find it a bit difficult, but I want to cook a lot of dishes.

Practice 2: Ohiru yasumi

Watashi no kaisha no chikaku ni konbini ga arimasu. Ohiru yasumi ni yoku konbini e ikimasu. Totemo benri desu.

Kyo wa 12 ji 45 fun goro ni ikimashita. Soshite Ohiru gohan o kaimashita. Onigiri to kudamono o kaimashita. Onigiri wa iroirona shurui ga arimasu. Kyo wa sake to ume o kaimashita. Totemo oishikatta desu.

* "ohiru yasumi" = lunch break

* "goro" = around

* "onigiri" = Japanese rice ball

* "iroirona" = various

* "shurui" = kind, type

* "sake" = salmon

* "ume" = umeboshi, salted plum

おひるやすみ

わたしの かいしゃの ちかく に コンビニ が あります。 おひる やすみに よく コンビニ へ いきます。 とても べんり です。

きょうは １２じ４５ふん ごろ に いきました。 そして おひるごはん を かいました。 おにぎり と くだもの を かいました。 おにぎり は いろいろな しゅるい が あります。 きょう は さけ と うめ を かいました。

とても おいしかった です。

Meaning:

Lunch Break

There is a convenience store near my office. I often go there during my lunch break.

It is very convenient for me.

Today I went there around 12:45, and bought some lunch. I bought onigiri and some fruits. There are many flavors for onigiri. Today I got salmon onigiri and ume onigiri.

They are very delicious.

Practice 3: Sukina dōga

Donna dōga ga suki desu ka?

Watashi wa dōbutsu no dōga ga suki desu.

Inu ya neko no dōga wo mimasu.

Totemo kawaii desu.

Watashi no kazoku no dōbutsu ga suki desu.

Sorede yoku bangohan no ato issho ni dōbutsu no dōga o mimasu

*dōga = video clips, short movies

*inu ya neko = dogs and cats

*〜no ato = after 〜

すきな どうが

どんな どうが が すき ですか。

わたし は どうぶつ の どうが が すきです。

いつも いぬ や ねこの どうが を みます。

とても かわいい です。

わたし の かぞく も どうぶつ が すき です。

それで よく ばんごはん の あと いっしょに どうぶつ の どうが を みます。

Meaning:

Favorite video

What kind of video do yo like?

I like videos of animals.

I always watch video of dogs and cats.

They are very cute.

My family likes animals, too.

So we often watch the video together after dinner.

Practice 4: Watashi no sumaho

Watashi no sumaho wa totemo furui desu. Soshite sikoshi osoi desu.

Shashin ga amari kirei dewa arimasen.

Atarashi sumaho wa shashin ga kirei desu.

Kurisumasu ni mise de se-ru ga arimasu.

Se-ru no toki ni atarashii sumaho o kaitai desu.

*~ no toki ni = when ~

わたし の スマホ

わたし の スマホ は とても ふるい です。

そして すこし おそい です。

しゃしん が あまり きれい では ありません。

あたらしい スマホ は しゃしん が きれい です。

クリスマス に みせで セール が あります。

セールの ときに あたらしい スマホ を かいたい です。

*~ no toki ni = when ~

Meaning:

My smart phone

My smart phone is very old, and a bit slow.

The photos that I can take with my phone are not that pretty.

New smartphones are very good with photos.

There is a Christmas sale at the shop.

I would like to buy a new smartphone during the sale.

Practice 5: Nihongo no benkyō

Kyō gakkō de hiragana to katakana to kanji o benkyō shimashita.

Hiragana to katakana wa mainichi kakimasu. Hiragana to katakana wa kanji yori kantan desu. Demo kanji no hō ga hiragana to katakana yori omoshiroi desu.

Watashi no sukina kanji wa "月" desu. Kono kanji no yomi wa "tsuki" desu.

Imi wa "moon" desu.

Korekara mo mainichi kanji o benkyō shimasu. Soshite kanji o takusan oboetai desu.

*"〜to〜 = 〜and 〜

* "yomi" = how to read

* "imi" = meaning

*"oboemasu" = to rememberr, to memorize

にほんご　の　べんきょう

きょう がっこう で ひらがな と カタカナ と　かんじ を べんきょうしました。

ひらがな と カタカナ を まいにち かきます。 ひらがな と かたかな は

かんじ より かんたん です。 でも かんじ の ほう が ひらがな と かたかな より

おもしろい です。 わたし の すきな かんじ は "月" です。

この かんじ のよみ は、 "つき" です。 いみ は、 "moon" です。

これから も まいにち かんじ を べんきょう します。

そして かんじ を たくさん おぼえたい です。

Meaning:

Studying Japanese

I studied hiragana, katakana, and kanji at school today.

I write hiragana and katakana every day. hiragana and katakana are easier than kanji.

But kanji is more interesting than hiragana and katakana.

My favorite kanji is "月". This kanji is read as "tsuki" and the meaning is "moon".

I want to learn kanji everyday from now on as well. I want to memorize many kanji.

Practice 6: Haru

Kyo kara 4 gatsu desu.

Kyo wa totemo atatakai ichinichi deshita.

Nihon no 4 gatsu wa sakura ga yūmei desu.

Hayaku sakura ga mitai desu. Wakuwaku shimasu.

4 gatsu kara atarashii gakkō ni ikimasu. Sakura mo gakkō mo tanoshimi desu.

April starting today.

In japan the sakura is famous in april.

I want to see sakura soon. I am starting a new school in april.

I am looking forward to both sakura and the new school.

* "haru" =spring

* "atatakai"= warm

* "tanoshimi" = looking forward to something

はる

きょう から 4がつ です。

きょう は とても あたたかい いちにち でした。

にほん の しがつは さくらが ゆうめいです。

さくらが みたいです。

しがつ から あたらしい がっこう が はじまります。さくら も がっこうも　　たのしみ です。

Meaning:

Spring

April starts today.

In Japan the sakura is famous in april.

I want to see sakura soon. I am starting a new school in april.

I am looking forward to both sakura and the new school.

Practice 7: Ryokō

Senshū tomodachi to kyōto ni ikimashita.

Tokyō kara Kyōto made Shinkansen de ikimashita.

Kyōto de oishii ryōri o takusan tabemashita.

Kireina Otera ga takusan arimashita. Kyōto wa sutekina machi deshita.

Shinkansen no naka kara fujisan o mimashita.

Fuji san wa nihon de ichiban takai yama desu.

Fuyu wa yama no ue ni yuki ga arimasu.

Yuki no fujisan mo kirei deshita.

Mata ikitai desu.

* "otera" = temple

* "yuki" = snow

* "mata" = again

りょこう

せんしゅう ともだち と きょうと に いきました。

とうきょう から きょうと まで しんかんせん で いきました。

きょうと で おいしい りょうり を たくさん たべました。

きれいな おてら や こうえん が たくさん ありました。

きょうと は すてきな まち でした。

しんかんせん の なか から ふじさん を みました。

ふじさん は にほん で いちばん たかい やま です。

ふゆ は やま の うえ に ゆき が あります。

ゆき の ふじさん も きれい でした。

また いきたい です。

Meaning:

Travelling

I went to kyoto with my friend last week.

I went from Tokyo to Kyōto by shinkansen/ bullet train.

In Kyoto we had delicious meals.

There were so many beautiful temples and parks.

Kyoto was a beautiful/ wonderful city.

From the shinkansen, I saw Mt Fuji.

Mt Fuji is the highest mountain in Japan.

In winter, we can see the snow on top of the mountain.

Mt Fuji with snow was very beautiful.

I want to go again.

Practice 8: Umi to Yama

Umi to Yama

A: B san wa umi to yama dochira ga suki desuka?

B: sō desu ne. Yama yori Umi no hou ga suki desu. Ie no chikaku ni umi ga arimasu.

Yoku umi ni ikimasu. Inu to Sanpo shimasu. Asa no umi wa totemo kirei desu yo. A san wa umi to yama dochira ga suki desuka/

A: watashi wa yama no hou ga suki desu. Shokubutsu ga suki desu. Sorede yoku yama ni ikimasu. Yama no kūki wa oishii desu yo.

B: ii desu ne. Kondo, yama ni ikitai desu.

A: raishū wa dō desu ka? Issho ni yama ni ikimasen ka?

B: Arigatou gozaimasu. Ikimashō.

* "umi" = ocean, sea

* "yama" = mountain

* "kuki" = air

うみ と やま

A: Bさん は うみ と やま、どちら が すき です か。

B: そう です ね。 やま より うみ の ほう が すき です。 いえ の ちかくに うみ が あります。 よく うみ に いきます。 いぬ と さんぽ を します。 あさ のうみ は とても きれい ですよ。Aさん は うみ と やま、どちら が すき です か。

A: わたし は やま の ほう が すき です。 しょくぶつ が すき です。 それで、よく やまに いきます。 やま の くうき は おいしい ですよ。

B: いい です ね。 こんど、 やま に いきたい です。

A: らいしゅう は どう です か。 いっしょ に やま に いきません か。

B: ありがとう ございます。 いっしょ に いきましょう。

Meaning:

Ocean and Mountain

A: Which one do you like better, ocean or mountain, B san?

B: Well, I like the ocean better than mountain. There is the ocean near my house. I often go there. I have a walk with my dog. The ocean in the morning is very beautiful. Which one do you like better, ocean or mountain, A san?

A: I like the mountains better. I like plants. Therefore, I often go to the mountain. The air in the mountain is fresh.

B: That sounds good. I want to go to the mountain next time.

How about next week? Won't you go to the mountain with me?

A : Thank you. Let's go together.

Answer Keys

Chapter 1

Exercise 1.1

kodomo こども

ie　いえ

Exercise 1.2

1) イタリア – g. ローマ	
2) ブラジル – h. リオデジャネイロ	
3) エジプト – a. カイロ	
4) インド　 – b. ニューデリー	
5) ベトナム – c. ホーチミン	
6) ポルトガル – d. リスボン	
7) フランス – e. パリ	
8) ロシア　– f. モスクワ ☐Check list #1 ☐ Tree ⇨ ki/ き ☐ Family ⇨ kazoku / かぞく ☐ Station ⇨ eki / えき ☐ Book ⇨ hon / ほん ☐ Study ⇨ benkyō / べんきょう ☐ Japanese language ⇨ nihon go / にほんご ☐ Friend ⇨ tomodachi/ ともだち ☐ Shop ⇨ mise / みせ	

Chapter 2

☑Check list #2

Can you answer the following questions?

☐ Sentence with topic marker "wa", will end with? ⇨ "desu"

☐ Topic marker which has a meaning of "also" ⇨ "mo"

☐ In negative sentence, "desu" changes to ? ⇨ "dewa arimasen"

☐ What does "ja arimasen" mean? ⇨ same as "dewa arimasen"

☐ How to say "yes" and "no" in japanese? ⇨ "hai" and "iie"

☐ What Japanese full stop looks like? ⇨ " 。 "

☑Check list #3

Can you say these greeting phrases in Japanese?

☐ "Nice to meet you" ⇨ "hajimemashite" (はじめまして)

☐ "Thank you" ⇨ "arigatō gozaimasu" (ありがとう ございます)

☐ "Good moring" ⇨ "ohayō gozaimasu" (おはよう ございます)

☐ "Hello" ⇨ "konnichiwa" (こんにちは)

☐ "Good night" ⇨ "oyasuminasai" (おやすみなさい)

☐ "Good evening" ⇨ "konbanwa" (こんばんは)

Exercise 2

1. maiku-san wa sensei desu ka? (Is Mike a teacher?)

2. watashi wa gakusei dewa arimasen (I am not a student.)

3. Anna-san mo gakusei desu (Anna is also a student.)

4. nihon jin dewa arimasen. (I'm not Japanese.)

Chapter 3

☑Check list #4

□ "The shop is big / wide." ⇨ みせ は おおきい です/ or ひろい です。

□ "Is the teacher kind?" ⇨ せんせい は しんせつ ですか。

□ "The child healthy / energetic." ⇨ こども は げんき です。

□ "Is Japanese difficult?" ⇨ にほんご は むずかしい ですか。

□ "Travelling is fun." ⇨ りょこう は たのしい です。

□ "Sushi is not yummy." ⇨ すし は おいしくない です。

Exercise 3

Identify the following whether it is i-adjective or na-adjective, and make the negative forms of each.

1. いそがしい です "isogashii desu" ⇨ i-adjective "isogashiku nai desu" いそがしくない です。

2. きれい です "kirei desu" ⇨ na-adjective "kirei dewa arimasen" きれい では ありません。

3. あつい です "atsui desu" ⇨ i-adjective "atsuku nai desu" あつく ない です。

4. ひま です "hima desu" ⇨ na-adjective "hima dewa arimasen" ひま では ありません。

5. いい です "ii desu" ⇨ i-adjective "yoku nai desu" よく ない です。

Chapter 4

☑Check list #5

Can you state the time below?

□3:40 ⇨ "san ji yon juppun" (さんじ よんじゅっぷん)

□4:50 am ⇨ " yoji go juppun"　(よじ　ごじゅっぷん)

□7:30 ⇨ "shichi ji han" or "shichi ji san juppun" (しちじ はん / さんじゅっぷん)

□8:25pm ⇨ " hachi ji niyū go fun" (はちじ にじゅうご ふん)

□9:45am ⇨ "gozen kuji yonjū go fun" (ごぜん くじ よんじゅうご ふん)

☑Check list #6

Can you say these prices?

□ ¥ 1200 ⇨ "sen ni hyaku en"　(せん にひゃく えん)

□ ¥ 13000 ⇨ "ichi man san zen en" (いち まん さん ぜん えん)

□ ¥ 8600 ⇨ " hassen roppyaku en" (はっせん ろっぴゃく えん)

□ ¥ 335 ⇨ " san byaku san jū go en" (さんびゃく さん じゅう ご えん)

□ ¥ 890 ⇨ "happyaku kyū jū en"　(はっぴゃく きゅうじゅう えん)

Exercises 4

1. Kyō wa getsu yōbi desu. (きょう は げつようび です。)　　⇨ "Today is Monday."

2. 10 gatsu 31 nichi wa kayōbi desu. (１０がつ３１にち は かようび です。) ⇨ "October 31st is Tuesday."

3. Konshū wa hima desu. (こんしゅう は ひま です。) ⇨ " I am free this week."

☑Check list #7

Can you say these phrases in Japanese?

□ "One to ten" ⇨ " ichi, ni, san, yon/ shi, go, roku, nana/ shichi, hachi, kyū/ ku, jū"

(いち, に ,さん, よん/ し, ご ,ろく, なな /しち, はち, きゅう/ く, じゅう)

☐ "What time is it? ⇨ "nan ji desu ka" (なんじ です か)

☐ "It's 4 o'clock" ⇨ "yo ji desu" (よじ です)

☐ "Today is tuesday." ⇨ " kyō wa kayōbi desu" (きょう は かようび です)

☐ "Tomorrow will be december 31st." ⇨ "ashita wa jūni gatsu san jū ichi nichi desu" (あした は じゅうに がつ さんじゅういち にち です   )

Chapter 5

☑Check list #8

Can you say these phrases in Japanese?

☐ "Here" ⇨ "koko" (ここ)

☐ "Where" ⇨ "doko" (どこ)

☐ "This one" ⇨ "kore" (これ)

☐ "That one is cheap." ⇨ "sore wa yasui desu." (それ は やすい です)

☐ "This is delicious." ⇨ "kore wa oishii desu." (これ は おいしい です)

☑Check list #9

Can you say these phrases or words in Japanese?

☐ "I like traveling." ⇨ "ryokō ga suki desu." (りょこう が すき です)

☐ "Who" ⇨ "dare" (だれ)

☐ "When" ⇨ "itsu" (いつ)

☐ "What kind of" ⇨ "donna" (どんな)

☐ "I do not like golf." ⇨ "gorufu ga suki dewa arimasen. / gorufu ga kirai desu."

(ゴルフ が すき では ありません / ゴルフ が きらい です)

Chapter 6

☑Check list #10

Can you say these phrases or words in Japanese?

☐ "From Monday to Friday" ⇨ "getsu yōbi kara kin yōbi made" (げつようび から きんようび まで)

☐ "Next week Saturday" ⇨ "raishū no do yōbi" (らいしゅう の どようび)

☐ "Me too" ⇨ "watashi mo" (わたし も)

☐ "Japanese book" ⇨ "nihongo no hon" (にほんご の ほん)

☐ "My friend's mother" ⇨ "tomodachi no okāsan" (ともだち の おかあさん)

☑Check list #11

Can you change these phrases to polite form / teinei-go? And check the meaning.

☐ "Arigatō" ⇨ "arigatō gozaimasu" (ありがとう ございます) = thank you very much

☐ "Namae" ⇨ "o namae" (おなまえ) = name / someone's name

☐ "Shigoto" ⇨ "o shigoto" (おしごと) = job / someone's job

☐ "Ryōri" ⇨ "o ryōri" (おりょうり) = meal / dish

☐ "Tanjōbi" ⇨ "o tanjōbi" (おたんじょうび) = birthday/ someone's borthday

☐ "Yoyaku" ⇨ "go yoyaku" (ごよやく) = reservation / someone's reservation

Chapter 7

Exercise 5

1. 11ji ni nemasu. (じゅういちじ に ねます。)

2. Nanji ni nemasuka? (なんじ に ねますか。)

3. Watashi wa kuji kara go-ji made hatarakimasu.

(わたしは くじから ごじはん まで はたらきます。)

4. Anna san wa getsuyōbi kara kinyōbi made hatarakimasu.

(アンナさんは げつようび から きんようび まで はたらきます。)

Exercise 6

Choose the appropriate particle for the sentences.

1. Hiragana o kakimasu. (ひらがな を かきます)

2. Tokyo ni ikimau. (とうきょう に いきます)

3. Nanji ni kaerimasu ka?(なんじ に かえります か)

4. 8 ji kara 9 ji made yasumimasu. (はちじ から くじ まで やすみます)

5. Eiga ga suki desu ka? (えいが が すき です か)

☑Check list #12

Can you say these phrases in Japanese?

☐ "Go shopping" ⇨ "kaimono ni ikimasu" (かいもの に いきます)

☐ "See / meet family" ⇨ "kazoku ni aimasu" (かぞく に あいます)

☐ "Go by subway" ⇨ "chikatetsu de ikimasu" (ちかてつ で いきます)

☐ "Read books" ⇨ "hon o yomimasu" (ほん を よみます)

☐ "Drink coffee" ⇨ "kōhī o nomimasu" (コーヒー を のみます)

□ "Talk with friends" ⇨ "tomodachi to hanashimasu" (ともだち と はなします)

Exercise 7

Here are the sentences for the schedule.

6 ji ni okimasu. 6ji han ni yoga o shimasu. 7ji ni asagohan o tabemasu. 9ji ni kaisha ni ikimasu. 9ji kara 12 ji made hatarakimasu. 12ji ha ni tomodachi ni aiimasu. 5ji ni basu de ie ni kaerimasu. 6ji kara 7ji made nihongo no benkyo o shimasu. 8 ji ni bangohan o tabemasu. 9ji kara 10 ji made hon o yomimasu. 11ji ni nemasu.

6じ に おきます。

6じはん に ヨガ をします。

7じ に あさごはん を たべます。

9じ に かいしゃ に いきます。

9じから 12じまで はたらきます。

12じはん に ともだち に あいます。

5じ に バスでいえに かえります。

6じから 7じまで にほんごの べんきょうを します。

8じ にばんごはんを たべます。

9じから 10じまで ほんを よみます。

11じ に ねます。

Exercise: 8

Change the ending of the sentence to the appropriate form.

1. Senshū ryokō ni (ikimasu) ⇨ ikimashita

2. Sakana o amari (tabemasu) ⇨ tabemasen

3. Kinō tomodachi wa (kimasu) ⇨ kimasen deshita *did not come

4. Kūkō ni zenzen (ikimasu) ⇨ ikimasen

5. Hirugohan wa (tabemasu) ⇨ tabemasen deshita * did not eat

Chapter 8

☑Check list #13

Can you say these greeting phrases in Japanese?

☐ "Right side of the bag" ⇨ "kaban no migi" (かばん の みぎ)

☐ "Near the house" ⇨ "ie no chikaku" "uchi no chikaku" (いえ の ちかく / うち の ちかく)

☐ "Outside of the station" ⇨ "eki no soto" (えき の そと)

☐ "Under the tree" ⇨ "ki no shita" (き の した)

☐ "In front of me" ⇨ "watashi no mae" (わたし の まえ)

☑Check list #14

Can you say these greeting phrases in Japanese?

☐ "It was hot today / Today was hot." ⇨ "kyo wa atsukatta desu"

(きょう は あつかったです。)

☐ "I bought 3 eggs." ⇨ "tamago wa mittsu (or sanko) kaimashita."

(たまご を みっつ/ さんこ かいました。)

☐ "Who is the most kind in your family?" ⇨ "kazoku de dare ga ichiban shinsetsu desu ka?"(かぞく で だれが いちばん しんせつ ですか。)

☐ "The movie was not interesting." ⇨ "eiga wa omoshiroku nakatta desu."

(えいが は おもしろくなかったです。)

☐ "I like summer better than winter." * summer = natsu / winter = fuyu ⇨ "natsu no hōga fuyu yori suki desu" "fuyu yori natsu no hō ga suki desu."

(なつのほうが ふゆより すきです。/ふゆより なつのほうが すきです。)

☑Check list ☐ #15

Can you say these greeting phrases in Japanese?

☐ "I want to go to Hokkaidō next year." ⇨ "Rainen Hokkaido ni ikitai desu."

(らいねん ほっかいどう に いきたい です。)

☐ "My sister wants to go home early." ⇨ "Imōto wa/ga hayaku ie ni kaeritagatte imasu."

(いもうと は/が はやく いえ に かえりたがっています。)

☐ "My friend wants a new bag." ⇨"tomodachi wa/ ga atarashii kaban o hoshigatte

Imasu." (ともだち は/が あたらしい かばん を ほしがっています。)

Chapter 9

☑Check list #16

Do you know the meaning of these phrases?

☐ "Wakarimasen" ⇨ "I do not understand"

☐ "Sumimasen" ⇨ "excuse me" "I am sorry"

☐ "Dōzo" ⇨ "please"

☐ "Onegai shimasu" ⇨ "please" "Please do"

☐ "Gomennasai" ⇨ "I am sorry"

☑Check list #17

Do you know the meaning of these phrases?

☐ "Dakara" ⇨ "so, therefore, consequently, that's why"

☐ "Demo" ⇨ "however, but, though, even though"

☐ "Soshite" ⇨ "and, and now, then"

☐ "Sorekara" ⇨ "and, after that, and then"

Japanese Phrasebook For Beginners: Learn Common Phrases In Context With Explanations For Everyday Use and Travel

Worldwide Nomad

Introduction

Welcome to your journey into the basics of Japanese! In this phrasebook, we're keeping things simple and practical to get you started on your conversations. No need to worry about complex grammar rules or overwhelming vocabulary—just focus on the essentials.

If you are traveling to Japan for the first time, use this as a guide to focus on everyday communication. We will go over the basics of travel, greetings, hotels, restaurants, and even phrases to use in case of emergencies. This phrasebook will be the key to enjoying your Japanese vacation without worry, and being able to communicate with the locals to have the best experience possible!

Chapter 1 – Greetings/etiquette

Note About Formal and Informal Language

Japanese places a lot of emphasis on formal interactions versus informal ones. When speaking or using Japanese, you will learn a few different ways to say the same thing whether you are in a polite or casual setting.

When you are speaking to coworkers, strangers, or anyone you don't have a close relationship with, you will use the formal versions of these phrases. If you are speaking to close friends or family, the language can be simplified and we will show you the phrases you can use to sound more casual. When in doubt always go with the more formal phrases!

Basic Words for Hello

Saying "hello" isn't so simple in Japanese, as there are many phrases that can be used to greet people. These differ depending on the time of the day.

The most basic phrase you have probably heard of is こんにちは which means "hello" but is mostly used in the afternoon.

Japanese	Furigana	Romaji	English
こんにちは	こんにちは	Konnichiwa	Hello

If you want to say hello to someone in the morning you would use the following phrase:

Japanese	Furigana	Romaji	English
おはようございます	おはよう ございます	Ohayou gozaimasu	Good morning

In the evening it would be こんばんは:

Japanese	Furigana	Romaji	English
こんばんは	こんばんは	Konbanwa	Good evening

Apart from those, when answering the phone in Japanese, there is a special phrase used. But this is exclusively used on the phone and never in person:

Japanese	Furigana	Romaji	English
もしもし	もし もし	Moshi moshi	Hello

You can also greet someone by asking how they have been:

Japanese	Furigana	Romaji	English
お元気ですか	おげんき です か	Ogenki desu ka	How are you?

When coming home after a day of being out, you will greet anyone home with a phrase that means "I'm back." This is a set phrase and goes with what the other person will say meaning "welcome home."

Japanese	Furigana	Romaji	English
ただいま	ただいま	Tadaima	I'm home

おかえり	おかえり	Okaeri	Welcome back

Introducing Yourself

There are a few simple ways to introduce yourself in Japanese. The easiest is to say your name, and then add the copula **です** (desu). This just means "I am X."

Japanese	Furigana	Romaji	English
ジョンです。	じょん です。	Jon desu.	I am John.

Of course, as we learned, this is a very casual way to introduce yourself. If you want to make it a little more polite you can say "My name is X."

Japanese	Furigana	Romaji	English
私の名前はジョンです。	わたし の なまえ は じょん です。	Watashi no namae wa Jon desu.	My name is John.

And there is an even more polite phrase you use that means the same as "I am X" but uses a more formal verb. This would be used in situations like the office, where you want to be more polite.

Japanese	Furigana	Romaji	English
初めまして、ジョンと申します。	はじめまして、じょんと もうします。	Hajimemashite, Jon to moushimasu.	Nice to meet you, I am John.

After introducing yourself in Japanese, it is polite to use the phrase よろしくお願いします (yoroshiku onegaishimasu) or the more formal どうぞよろしくお願いします (douzo yoroshiku onegaishimasu). This phrase doesn't have a set translation in English. It is usually translated as "please be kind to me" but it is used in various situations, usually at the end of a polite interaction Once you learn the different situations this phrase can be used in, you will get the hang of when and where to say it. For right now, just remember it is usually said after introducing yourself to someone.

Japanese	Furigana	Romaji	English
どうぞよろしくお願いします。	どうぞ よろしく おねがい します。	Douzo yoroshiku onegaishimasu.	Please be kind to me / Nice to meet you.

Bowing as a Greeting

In Japan, it is still common to bow as you meet someone. Some international businesses will use a handshake, but bowing is still standard.

For men, keep your hands at your sides, and for women, hold your hand in front of you while you bow.

The general rule is the longer and deeper the bow, the more respect it signifies to the person you are greeting. So you might bow lower to the president of your company, but just give a slight head nod to a classmate.

Honorifics in Japanese

If you have any experience with Japanese you probably have heard someone use "san" or "chan" at the end of a person's name. These are called honorifics and there are a few common ones you should learn when starting to speak Japanese. Using someone's name without an honorific is very informal, so especially when you first meet someone, remember to use honorifics to avoid any uncomfortable feelings.

〜さん (-san) is the general polite honorific and is the standard to use when you don't know someone well. This can be used for strangers, coworkers, mutual friends, and people you just met. San can be used for anyone regardless of gender.

Japanese	Furigana	Romaji	English
お誕生日おめでとうございます、山田さん。	おたんじょうびおめでとうございます、やまださん。	Otanjoubi omedetou gozaimasu, Yamada-san.	Happy birthday, Mr./Ms. Yamada.

Next is the more formal "sama" which is used for people who are in a much higher position than you. If you talk to your company's president or are meeting your girlfriend's grandparents, you would use sama. Sama is also used for customers, so don't be alarmed if your hairdresser or other service people use sama when addressing you.

Japanese	Furigana	Romaji	English
山田様、お手紙を頂きまして誠にありがとうございます。	やまださま、おてがみ を いただきまして まことに ありがとうございます。	Yamada-sama, otegami o itadakimashite makoto ni arigatou gozaimasu.	Mr./Ms. Yamada, thank you very much for your letter.

Chan is an honorific used for young children, female adolescents, and sometimes close friends. Any time you see a very young child you can use chan, and you will often hear adults use chan when they meet other people's kids. Anything "cute" can use chan, including small animals. In fact, Hello Kitty in Japan is called "Kitty-chan." Girls, sometimes up until their teens, will use chan with each other as well. Finally, very close adult friends, family, and people in relationships sometimes use chan to show closeness and affection.

Japanese	Furigana	Romaji	English
もも、おばあちゃんちに行こうよ！	もも、おばあちゃんち に いこうよ！	Momo, obaachan chi ni ikou yo!	Momo, let's go to Grandma's!

Kun is also used for children, but only boys, and can be used until adolescence. It is most often used by those of the same age or by superiors addressing their subordinates It is very informal so using it in friendly and casual situations is best.

Japanese	Furigana	Romaji	English
誠くん、お昼ご飯一緒に食べない？	まことくん、おひるごはん いっしょに たべない？	Makoto-kun, ohiru gohan issho ni tabenai?	Makoto-kun, do you want to have lunch together?

Sensei is used for teachers, professors, and doctors. It is an honorific used to show respect for an authority figure who is teaching you something.

Japanese	Furigana	Romaji	English
先生、質問があります。	せんせい、しつもん が あります。	Sensei, shitsumon ga arimasu.	Teacher, I have a question.

Senpai and kouhai are honorifics used in a unique relationship in Japan, in which an older student or superior takes on an underling as a kind of mentor program. This usually happens in schools in which the older students help the younger ones, in student clubs or sports, and even in office settings in which an older employee will take on a newer one to show them the ropes. They can be used as honorifics, or just in place of the person's name.

Japanese	Furigana	Romaji	English
先輩、アドバイスをいただけますか？	せんぱい、あどばいす を いただけますか？	Senpai, adobaisu o itadakemasu ka?	Senpai, could you give me some advice?

Saying Goodbye

We went over how to say hello and introduce ourselves, but at the end of a meeting, we also need to learn how to say goodbye. Here are a few common phrases used to say goodbye to someone.

Japanese	Furigana	Romaji	English
さようなら。	さようなら。	Sayonara.	Goodbye.
じゃね！	じゃね！	Ja ne!	See you!
またね。	またね。	Mata ne.	See you again.
バイバイ。	ばいばい。	Bai bai.	Bye-bye.
また明日。	また あした。	Mata ashita.	See you tomorrow.

At the end of a work day, there is a common phrase used to thank coworkers and employees for their hard work. It means something close to "you are tired" but is used as a goodbye and a thank you for putting in a full work day. You can use this when saying bye to anyone at the office.

Japanese	Furigana	Romaji	English
お疲れ様でした。	おつかれさま でした。	Otsukaresama deshita.	Thank you for your hard work.

When leaving home there is a set phrase, much like "tadaima" and "okaeri" from earlier that means "I'm home" and "welcome back". These phrases are used to say, "I'm off" to let your family or friends know you are leaving, and "Go and come back" to say you hope they return.

Japanese	Furigana	Romaji	English
行ってきます。	いってきます。	Ittekimasu.	I'm off.
行ってらっしゃい。	いってらっしゃい。	Itterasshai.	Go and come back.

Chapter 2 - Public transportation

Transportation in Japan

Japan is known for its highly efficient and punctual transportation systems compared to some other countries. All major cities have buses, trains, and shuttles to take you to any tourist spots you want to visit. Stations in big cities like Tokyo and Osaka will have almost everything in English so you will have no trouble navigating your way around. However, smaller towns in Japan will often have no English, so learning how to say some basic phrases in Japanese will go a long way.

Buying Tickets

Tickets for most trains and some buses can be purchased directly at the window with the Station Attendant, or in specified ticket vending machines. On most buses or shorter transports like cable cars or street cars, you can also purchase tickets directly on the bus, or even simply pay in cash as you get off. IC cards are also becoming a popular option, which you can recharge online and tap the sensors as you get on or off different types of transportation. But although technology is catching up in the big cities, rural Japan is still very much a cash-based society, so be sure to have cash on hand when you are traveling in the countryside!

When you are ready to buy your ticket, here are a few phrases to help you:

Japanese	Furigana	Romaji	English
切符を買いたいんです が。	きっぷを かいたいん です が。	Kippu o kaitain desu ga.	I would like to buy a ticket.
指定席を予約したいです。	していせき を よやく したい です。	Shiteiseki o yoyaku shitai desu.	I would like to reserve a reserved seat.
自動券売機はどこ ですか？	じどう けんばい き は どこ ですか？	Jidou kenbai ki wa doko desu ka?	Where is the ticket vending machine?

大人と子供の切符をください。	おとな と こども の きっぷ を ください。	Otona to kodomo no kippu o kudasai.	A child and adult ticket, please.
このバスの運賃はいくらですか？	この ばす の うんちん は いくら ですか？	Kono basu no unchin wa ikura desu ka?	How much is the fare for this bus?
IC カードで支払えますか？	いーしー かーど で しはらえます か？	IC kaado de shiharaemasu ka?	Can I pay with an IC card?
学割がありますか？	がくわり が あります か？	Gakuwari ga arimasu ka?	Is there a student discount?
運転中に切符を買えますか？	うんてん ちゅう に きっぷ を かえます か？	Unten-chuu ni kippu o kaemasu ka?	Can I buy a ticket while on the train?

Payment and IC Cards

Paying for transportation can still be done in cash almost everywhere in Japan. But today IC cards are becoming a more popular choice. The big companies for IC cards in Japan are ICOCA, Pasmo, and Suica. With these companies, you can usually buy a card and charge it online. Then you simply tap the card when entering and leaving a station to make your payment. Here are a few phrases to help you talk about using an IC in Japanese:

Japanese	Furigana	Romaji	English
IC カードで乗り降りできます。	いーしー かーど で のりおり できます。	IC kaado de noriori dekimasu.	You can board and exit using an IC card.

新しい IC カードを作りたいんですが、どこでできますか？	あたらしい いーしー かーど を つくりたい ん です が、 どこ で できます か？	Atarashii IC kaado o tsukuritai ndesu ga, doko de dekimasu ka?	I want to make a new IC card; where can I do that?
IC カードの残高が足りないときはどうしたらいいですか？	いーしー かーど の ざんだか が たりない とき は どう したら いい です か？	IC kaado no zandaka ga tarinai toki wa dou shitara ii desu ka?	What should I do if my IC card balance is low?
この IC カードは他の乗り物でも使えますか？	この いーしー かーど は ほか の のりもの でも つかえます か？	Kono IC kaado wa hoka no norimono demo tsukaemasu ka?	Can I use this IC card for other transportation?
電車を乗り換えるとき、IC カードをどうやって使いますか？	でんしゃ を のりかえる とき、 いーしー かーど を どう やって つかいます か？	Densha o norikaeru toki, IC kaado o dou yatte tsukaimasu ka?	How do I use the IC card when transferring trains?
列車に乗る前に、IC カードをタッチしてください。	れっしゃ に のる まえ に、 いーしー かーど を たっち して ください。	Ressha ni noru mae ni, IC kaado o tacchi shite kudasai.	Before getting on the train, please touch your IC card.

Asking for Directions

Even the best of us get lost sometimes! Especially if this is your first time in Japan and you are visiting places like Tokyo, where the map of the subway can be confusing and overwhelming. Prepare yourself by being able to ask some specific questions about how to get around on public transit.

The station attendant usually stands in a little office on the side of the ticket gate and is willing to help you with any questions you might have. But many passengers are also willing to help if the station attendants are unavailable.

Japanese	Furigana	Romaji	English
駅はどこですか？	えき は どこ です か？	Eki wa doko desu ka?	Where is the station?
この電車はどこ行きですか？	この でんしゃ は どこ いきですか？	Kono densha wa doko iki desu ka?	Where does this train go?
どうやってバス停に行けますか？	どうやって ばすてい に いけますか？	Dou yatte basutei ni ikemasu ka?	How do I get to the bus stop?
このバスはどのくらいかかりますか？	この ばす は どのくらい かかりますか？	Kono basu wa dono kurai kakarimasu ka?	How much does this bus cost?
新宿駅までの行き方を教えてください。	しんじゅくえき まで の いきかた を おしえて ください。	Shinjuku eki made no ikikata o oshiete kudasai.	Can you tell me how to get to Shinjuku Station?
この電車で東京駅に行けますか？	この でんしゃ で とうきょうえき に いけますか？	Kono densha de Tokyo eki ni ikemasu ka?	Can I go to Tokyo Station on this train?
どのホームから新大阪行きの電車が出ますか？	どの ほーむ から しんおおさかゆき の でんしゃ が でますか？	Dono homu kara Shin-Osaka yuki no densha ga demasu ka?	Which platform does the train to Shin-Osaka leave from?

この地下鉄は浜松町まで行きますか？	この ちかてつ は はままつちょう まで いきます か？	Kono chikatetsu wa Hamamatsucho made ikimasu ka?	Does this subway go to Hamamatsucho?

Station Signs and Displays

A Japanese bus or train station can be overwhelming if you are in a big city and there is a ton of kanji surrounding you for the first time. But don't panic! Here are some signs and displays you might see in the station, so study them and be prepared when you ride on public transit in Japan.

Japanese	Furigana	Romaji	English
改札口	かいさつぐち	Kaisatsuguchi	Ticket Gate
ホーム	ほーむ	Houmu	Platform
乗り換え口	のりかえぐち	Norikaeguchi	Transfer Gate
出口	でぐち	Deguchi	Exit
案内	あんない	Annai	Information
時刻表	じこくひょう	Jikokuhyou	Timetable
券売機	けんばいき	Kenbaiki	Ticket Vending Machine
自動改札機	じどうかいさつき	Jidoukaisatsuki	Automatic Ticket Gate
乗り場	のりば	Noriba	Boarding Place

エレベーター	えれべーたー	Erebeetaa	Elevator
トイレ	といれ	Toire	Toilet
発車口	はっしゃぐち	Hasshaguchi	Departure Gate
到着口	とうちゃくぐち	Touchakuguchi	Arrival Gate
指定席	していせき	Shiteiseki	Reserved Seat
自由席	じゆうせき	Jiyuuseki	Unreserved Seat
特急	とっきゅう	Tokkyuu	Express
快速	かいそく	Kaisoku	Rapid

Priority Seating

On all trains and buses, you will see a space reserved for priority passengers.

Japanese	Furigana	Romaji	English
優先席	ゆうせんせき	Yuusen-seki	Priority Seating

When you see this sign, make sure you give up your seat to any passengers who may need it. In Japan, these seats are usually for elderly passengers, passengers with disabilities, pregnant women, or those with children. If the seats are available feel free to sit in them, but be aware if another passenger might need to use them. Here are a few polite ways to offer your seat to someone on the train or bus:

Japanese	Furigana	Romaji	English
どうぞ、座ってください。	どうぞ、すわってください。	Douzo, suwatte kudasai.	Please, have a seat.
座っていただけますか？	すわっていただけますか？	Suwatte itadakemasu ka?	Would you like to take a seat?
どうぞ、この席は空いています。	どうぞ、このせきはあいています。	Douzo, kono seki wa aiteimasu.	Please, this seat is available.
ご自由にどうぞ。	ごじゆうにどうぞ。	Gojiyuu ni douzo.	Please feel free to take it.

Delays and Cancellations

Although Japanese public transportation is almost always on time, there are a few situations in which a train or bus will be delayed or even canceled. This includes inclement weather, earthquakes, or accidents on the tracks. Here are a few announcements you might hear when you are on the train or the platform about delays and cancellations.

Japanese	Furigana	Romaji	English
ご乗車の皆様へ、大変申し訳ございませんが、運転を見合わせさせていただきます。	ごじょうしゃのみなさまへ、たいへんもうしこみございませんが、うんてん を みあわせ させていただきます。	Gojousha no minasama e, taihen moushikomi gozaimasen ga, unten o miawase sasete itadakimasu.	To all passengers, we sincerely apologize, but we will temporarily suspend operations.

急なトラブルにより、列車は遅れております。	きゅうな とらぶる により、れっしゃ は おくれて おります。	Kyuu na toraburu ni yori, ressha wa okurete orimasu.	Due to unforeseen issues, the train is delayed.
本日のバスは欠航となりました。予めご了承ください。	ほんじつ の ばす は けっこう と なりました。 あらかじめ ごりょうしょう ください。	Honjitsu no basu wa kekkou to narimashita. Arakajime goryoushou kudasai.	Today's bus has been canceled. Please be aware in advance.
突発的な事態により、列車は一時停車となります。	とっぱつてき な じたい により、れっしゃ は いちじ ていしゃ と なります。	Toppatsuteki na jitai ni yori, ressha wa ichiji teisha to narimasu.	Due to an unexpected situation, the train will come to a temporary stop.
バスの運行が中止となりました。ご迷惑をおかけして誠に申し訳ありません。	ばす の うんこう が ちゅうし と なりました。 ごめいわく を おかけ して まこと に もうしこみ ありません。	Basu no unkou ga chuushi to narimashita. Gomeiwaku o okake shite makoto ni moushikomi arimasen.	Bus services have been suspended. We sincerely apologize for the inconvenience.

Useful Vocabulary for Transportation

Japanese	Furigana	Romaji	English
電車	でんしゃ	(Densha)	Train

バス	ばす	(Basu)	Bus
駅	えき	(Eki)	Station
地下鉄	ちかてつ	(Chikatetsu)	Subway
タクシー	たくしー	(Takushii)	Taxi
レンタカー	れんたかー	(Rentakaa)	Rental car
道路	どうろ	(Douro)	Road
航空機	こうくうき	(Koukuuki)	Airplane
空港	くうこう	(Kuukou)	Airport
乗り換え	のりかえ	(Norikae)	Transfer (between trains, buses, etc.)
運賃	うんちん	(Unchin)	Fare
切符	きっぷ	(Kippu)	Ticket
乗車券	じょうしゃけん	(Joushaken)	Boarding pass
遅延	ちえん	(Chien)	Delay
発車	はっしゃ	(Hassha)	Departure
到着	とうちゃく	(Touchaku)	Arrival

止まる	とまる	(Tomaru)	To stop (for a vehicle)
発車する	はっしゃする	(Hassha suru)	To depart
到着する	とうちゃくする	(Touchaku suru)	To arrive
運転手	うんてんしゅ	(Untenshu)	Driver
降りる	おりる	(Oriru)	To get off (a vehicle)

Chapter 3 - Lodging, hotels

Hotels in Japan

For your first time in Japan, you will probably be staying in a hotel. Hotels in Japan have a few differences from those in other countries, so learning Japanese words and phrases that will help you acclimate to a Japanese hotel is essential.

Arrival and Check-in

When you arrive at a Japanese hotel, it's best to have a reservation, as most room reservations are made online or over the phone and hotels especially in major cities fill up fast. General hotels will either be a Western type or a traditional Japanese inn called a 旅館 (りょかん, ryokan). These tend to have Japanese-style rooms with shared public baths that might be different from the hotels you are used to. Here are some phrases to help you with arriving and checking in to your hotel.

Japanese	Furigana	Romaji	English
こんにちは、予約をしています。	こんにちは、よやくを しています。	Konnichiwa, yoyaku o shiteimasu.	Hello, I have a reservation.
チェックインの時間は何時ですか？	チェックイン の じかん は なんじ ですか？	Chekkuin no jikan wa nanji desu ka?	What time is check-in?
お名前と予約名を教えてください。	おなまえ と よやくめい を おしえて ください。	Onamae to yoyaku mei o oshiete kudasai.	Please tell me your name and reservation details.
パスポートとクレジットカードをご提示ください。	パスポート と くれじっとかーど を ごていじょう ください。	Pasupooto to kurejitto kaado o go-teijou kudasai.	Please present your passport and credit card.

Wi-Fi のパスワードを教えていただけますか？	わい ふぁい の ぱすわーどを おしえて いただけますか？	Wai fai no pasuwaado o oshiete itadakemasu ka?	Could you please tell me the Wi-Fi password?

Hotel Room Facilities and Amenities

Japanese hotel rooms are a little different than those in other countries. To start, Japanese hotels are usually much smaller. Most hotels are used simply as a place to sleep, so especially for business hotels will be little more than a bed and desk, with very little space to stretch out. Of course, more luxury hotels will have bigger rooms, but they are still usually smaller than other countries.

There will also be an entranceway called a "genkan" where you will remove your shoes before entering. Japanese people always remove their shoes while in the house, so staying in a hotel is no different.

If you are staying at a Japanese-style inn you might find a small room with tatami mat or straw mat flooring. In these rooms, the bedding is kept in the closet and laid out on the floor when it is time to sleep.

Also in some Japanese hotels, the toilet and bath areas are separated into two different rooms.

Japanese	Furigana	Romaji	English
ホテルの部屋に入りましょう。	ほてる の へやに はいりましょう。	Hoteru no heya ni hairimashou.	Let's enter the hotel room.
日本のホテルの部屋は小さいです。	にほん の ほてる の へや は ちいさいです。	Nihon no hoteru no heya wa chiisai desu.	Japanese hotel rooms are small.
玄関で靴を脱ぎましょう。	げんかん で くつ を ぬぎましょう。	Genkan de kutsu o hagimashou.	Let's remove our shoes in the entranceway.

Navigating the Hotel

Hotels often have a staff that can help you with anything you need during your stay. Here are some phrases you might want to use to ask them questions about the hotel and surrounding areas:

Japanese	Furigana	Romaji	English
朝食は何時からですか？	ちょうしょく は なんじ から です か？	Choushoku wa nanji kara desu ka?	What time is breakfast?
レストランの場所を教えてください。	れすとらん の ばしょ を おしえてください。	Resutoran no basho o oshiete kudasai.	Please tell me the location of the restaurant.
観光地のおすすめはありますか？	かんこうち の おすすめ は あります か？	Kankouchi no osusume wa arimasu ka?	Do you have any recommendations for tourist attractions?
ホテル周辺にコンビニはありますか？	ほてる しゅうへん に こんびに は あります か？	Hoteru shuuhen ni konbini wa arimasu ka?	Is there a convenience store around the hotel?
地図を見せていただけますか？	ちず を みせて いただけます か？	Chizu o misete itadakemasu ka?	Could you show me the map?
空港へのシャトルバスはありますか？	くうこう へ の しゃとるばす は あります か？	Kuukou e no shatorubasu wa arimasu ka?	Is there a shuttle bus to the airport?

| ホテルの周りにレストランはありますか？ | ほてる の まわり に れすとらん は ありますか？ | Hoteru no mawari ni resutoran wa arimasu ka? | Are there restaurants around the hotel? |

Check-out

Japanese	Furigana	Romaji	English
おはようございます、チェックアウトの時間は何時ですか？	おはようございます、ちぇっくあうとの じかん は なんじ ですか？	Ohayou gozaimasu, chekkuauto no jikan wa nanji desu ka?	Good morning, what time is check-out?
お名前と部屋番号を教えてください。	おなまえと へやばんごう を おしえて ください。	Onamae to heya bangou o oshiete kudasai.	Please tell me your name and room number.
領収書をお願いします。	りょうしゅうしょ を おねがい します。	Ryoushuusho o onegai shimasu.	Please provide a receipt.
お部屋の鍵を返却させていただきます。	おへや の かぎ を へんきゃく させて いただきます。	Oheya no kagi o henkyaku sasete itadakimasu.	I will return the room key.
忘れ物がないか、部屋を最後にチェックさせてください。	わすれもの が ない か、へや を さいご に ちぇっく させて ください。	Wasuremono ga nai ka, heya o saigo ni chekku sasete kudasai.	Please let me check the room one last time for any forgotten items.

| またのご利用をお待ちしております。 | また の ごりよう を おまち して おります。 | Mata no goriyou o omachi shite imasu. | We look forward to serving you again. |

Useful Vocabulary for Lodging and Hotels

Japanese	Furigana	Romaji	English
ホテル	ほてる	(hoteru)	Hotel
予約	よやく	(yoyaku)	Reservation/Booking
フロント	ふろんと	(furonto)	Front desk
チェックイン	ちえっくいん	(chekkuin)	Check-in
チェックアウト	ちえっくあうと	(chekkuauto)	Check-out
部屋	へや	(heya)	Room
Wi-Fi	わいふぁい	(wai fai)	Wi-Fi
レストラン	れすとらん	(resutoran)	Restaurant
清掃	せいそう	(seisou)	Housekeeping/Cleaning
エレベーター	えれべーたー	(erebeetaa)	Elevator

トイレ	といれ	(toire)	Toilet
非常口	ひじょうぐち	(hijouguchi)	Emergency exit
案内	あんない	(annai)	Information/Guide
キャンセル	きゃんせる	(kyanseru)	Cancel
料金	りょうきん	(ryoukin)	Fee/Charge
禁煙	きんえん	(kin'en)	No smoking
エアコン	えあこん	(eakon)	Air conditioning

Chapter 4 - Food and restaurants

Types of Restaurants

There are a few different types of restaurants in Japan, and depending on what you want to eat and what environment you are looking for, you will want to know the vocabulary for each one.

Japanese	Furigana	Romaji	English
居酒屋	いざかや	Izakaya	Pub

This is a casual Japanese pub that serves a variety of small dishes, similar to tapas. Often popular for after-work gatherings and casual socializing.

Japanese	Furigana	Romaji	English
ラーメン屋	らーめんや	Raamenya	Ramen Restaurant

Specializes in ramen, a popular Japanese noodle soup dish. Ramen shops can have different styles of broth, noodles, and toppings.

Japanese	Furigana	Romaji	English
寿司屋	すしや	Sushiya	Sushi Restaurant

Focuses on sushi, a traditional Japanese dish consisting of vinegared rice combined with various ingredients such as seafood, vegetables, and occasionally tropical fruits.

Japanese	Furigana	Romaji	English
懐石料理	かいせきりょうり	Kaisekiryouri	Kaiseki Cuisine

Offers a multi-course meal that highlights seasonal ingredients and meticulous presentation. Kaiseki is often considered a traditional and formal dining experience.

Japanese	Furigana	Romaji	English
鉄板焼き屋	てっぱんやきや	Teppanyaki-ya	Teppanyaki Restaurant

Features teppanyaki, a style of cooking where chefs grill ingredients like meat and vegetables on an iron griddle right in front of the diners.

Japanese	Furigana	Romaji	English
ファミリーレストラン	ふぁみりーれすとらん	Famiri resutoran	Family Restaurant

A larger diner-style restaurant opened in the afternoons with large menus and a variety of choices. It is popular for cheap food and families with children who want to enjoy a restaurant.

Making a Reservation

Although some restaurants now have online options available for making a reservation, most still primarily use the phone. So if you want to make a reservation at a Japanese restaurant, then you will need to be familiar with a few words and phrases to help you navigate speaking on the phone.

Japanese	Furigana	Romaji	English

予約をしたいんですが。	よやく を したいんです が。	Yoyaku o shitain desu ga.	I'd like to make a reservation.
何人でしょうか。	なんにん でしょうか。	Nannin deshou ka.	How many people?
今日の夜、8時にお願いします。	きょう の よる、はちじ に おねがいします。	Kyou no yoru, hachiji ni onegaishimasu.	Tonight at 8 o'clock, please.
禁煙席でお願いします。	きんえんせき で おねがいします。	Kinen-seki de onegaishimasu.	Non-smoking, please.
窓際の席がいいです。	まどぎわ の せき が いい です。	Madogiwa no seki ga ii desu.	I'd like a window seat.
特別なリクエストはありますか。	とくべつ な りくえすと は ありますか。	Tokubetsu na rikuesuto wa arimasu ka.	Any special requests?
キャンセルがあればお知らせください。	きゃんせる が あれば おしらせ ください。	Kyanseru ga areba oshirase kudasai.	Please let us know if there's a cancellation.
名前を教えていただけますか。	なまえ を おしえて いただけます か。	Namae o oshiete itadakemasu ka.	Could you tell us your name?
予約は確認しました。	よやく は かくにん しました。	Yoyaku wa kakunin shimashita.	Your reservation has been confirmed.

お誕生日ですか。特別なお祝いはありますか。	おたんじょうび ですか。とくべつな おいわい は ありますか。	Otanjoubi desu ka. Tokubetsu na oiwai wa arimasu ka.	Is it a birthday? Any special celebration?

Ordering

In Japan, it's customary for waitstaff to leave you alone at the table until you call them. And to call them you can yell "Excuse me!" or すみません (sumimasen) loudly in the restaurant to get their attention. This might seem rude to Westerners, but it is perfectly acceptable to yell loudly to get the attention of the waitstaff.

Japanese	Furigana	Romaji	English
メニューを見せていただけますか。	めにゅう を みせて いただけます か。	Menyuu o misete itadakemasu ka.	Could you show me the menu?
これをお願いします。	これ を おねがいします。	Kore o onegaishimasu.	I'll have this, please.
お勧めは何ですか。	おすすめ は なん です か。	Osusume wa nan desu ka.	What do you recommend?
辛いのは苦手です。	からい の は にがて です。	Karai no wa nigate desu.	I'm not good with spicy food.
お水をお願いします。	おみず を おねがいします。	Omizu o onegaishimasu.	Water, please.
アレルギーがあります。	あれるぎー が あります。	Arerugii ga arimasu.	I have allergies.

トイレはどこです か。	トイレ は どこ です か。	Toire wa doko desu ka.	Where is the restroom?
お会計お願いしま す。	おかいけい おねがいします。	Okaikei onegaishimasu.	The check, please.
別の皿をください 。	べつ の さら を ください。	Betsu no sara o kudasai.	Can I have a separate plate?
テイクアウトはで きますか。	ていくあうと は できます か。	Teikuauto wa dekimasu ka.	Is takeout available?
ご飯は無料ですか 。	ごはん は むりょう です か。	Gohan wa muryou desu ka.	Is rice complimentary?
これは辛いですか 。	これ は からい です か。	Kore wa karai desu ka.	Is this spicy?
お箸を使ってもい いですか。	おはし を つかって も いい です か。	Ohashi o tsukatte mo ii desu ka.	Is it okay to use chopsticks?
デザートもお願い します。	でざーと も おねがいします。	Dezaato mo onegaishimasu.	Dessert, please.

Dining Etiquette

Dining etiquette in Japanese can be complicated, but if you keep in mind a few simple rules you are sure not to offend anyone around you. Firstly, simple table manners are observed, like not putting your elbows on the table and not chewing with your mouth open.

Japanese	Furigana	Romaji	English

スープをすするのは大丈夫です。	すーぷ を すする の は だいじょうぶ です。	Suupu o susuru no wa daijoubu desu.	It's okay to slurp soup.
食事中に携帯電話を使用しないでください。	しょくじちゅう に けいたいでんわ を しようしないで ください。	Shokuji chuu ni keitai denwa o shiyoushinaide kudasai.	Please do not use your mobile phone during the meal.
お盆に手を乗せないでください。	おぼん に て を のせないで ください。	Obon ni te o nose naide kudasai.	Please do not place your hands on the tray.
食事前に、おしぼりを使って手を拭いてください。	しょくじまえに、お しぼり を つかって て を ふいて ください。	Shokuji mae ni, nureta oshibori o tsukatte te o fuite kudasai.	Please use the wet towel to wipe your hands before eating.

Before the meal Japanese people will typically put their hands together like they are about to pray and say their version of "bon appetite" which literally means "I will receive." This can also be said before different courses like dessert when it comes out later in the meal.

Japanese	Furigana	Romaji	English
いただきます。	いただきます。	Itadakimasu.	Bon appétit.

When you are finished with a meal you say thank you by using the following phrase. Though it literally means "I had a feast" it is used to thank the people you are with, or the restaurant as you are leaving. It is also perfectly fine to yell this to staff as you walk out of the door.

Japanese	Furigana	Romaji	English
ご馳走さまでした。	ごちそうさまでした。	Gochisousama deshita.	Thank you for the meal.

There are a few points of etiquette to highlight when using chopsticks. Since chopsticks are an important tool used in Japanese funerals, there are a few things you need to avoid so the people around you aren't reminded of funeral rites. The first is to never stick your chopsticks into the rice to rest them. In between using chopsticks, make sure to set them on the chopstick rest at your table. If there is no rest, them setting them down on the side of your plate or bowl is fine.

You also want to avoid passing anything from chopstick to chopstick, as this is done with the bones of loved ones in a traditional Japanese funeral. If you need to pass food to someone, set the foot down on their plate in front of them, and let them pick it up with their own chopsticks.

Lastly, if there is shared food at the table, don't use the chopsticks that you have been using to serve yourself. Either use a separate pair of chopsticks or a spoon provided for serving. If those are not available, you can use the opposite end of your chopsticks to grab communal food from the table.

Japanese	Furigana	Romaji	English
お箸をテーブルに突き立てないでください。	おはし を てーぶる に つきたて ないで ください。	Ohashi o teeburu ni tsukitate naide kudasai.	Please don't stick chopsticks into the rice.
これを渡していただけますか。	これ を わたして いただけます か。	Kore o watashite itadakemasu ka.	Can you pass me this?
もう一つ小皿をいただけますか。	もう ひとつ こざら を いただけます か。	Mou hitotsu kozara o itadakemasu ka.	Can I get another small plate?
箸置きはありますか。	はしおき は あります か。	Hashioki wa arimasu ka.	Is there a chopstick rest?

Paying and Leaving

When you are ready to leave, call over the waitstaff once again and ask for the check to go. Most payment in Japan is still done with cash, but cards and other form of payment are becoming more popular. Most restaurants do not allow you to take food home, so sometimes they will not have a box or bag available if you don't finish your food. Thankfully, Japanese food comes in small portions so you will usually not have any leftovers.

Japanese	Furigana	Romaji	English
お会計お願いします。	おかいけい おねがいします。	Okaikei onegaishimasu.	The check, please.
カードで支払ってもいいですか。	かーど で しはらって も いい です か。	Kādo de shiharatte mo ii desu ka.	Can I pay with a card?
これでお願いします。	これ で おねがいします。	Kore de onegaishimasu.	I'll pay with this.
お釣りはいりません。	おつり は いりません。	Otsuri wa irimasen.	I don't need change.
ありがとうございました。	ありがとう ございました。	Arigatou gozaimashita.	Thank you very much.
またお伺いします。	また おうかがい します。	Mata oukagai shimasu.	I'll come again.
お持ち帰りできますか。	おもちかえり できます か。	Omochikaeri dekimasu ka.	Can I get this to go?

Useful Vocabulary for Food and Restaurants

Japanese	Furigana	Romaji	English
食べ物	たべもの	Tabemono	Food
料理	りょうり	Ryouri	Cuisine, Dish
飲み物	のみもの	Nomimono	Drink
メニュー	めにゅー	Menyuu	Menu
注文	ちゅうもん	Chuumon	Order
お水	おみず	Omizu	Water
ご飯	ごはん	Gohan	Rice
お茶	おちゃ	Ocha	Tea
おしぼり	おしぼり	Oshibori	Wet Towel
スープ	すーぷ	Suupu	Soup
刺身	さしみ	Sashimi	Sliced Raw Fish
寿司	すし	Sushi	Sushi
味噌汁	みそしる	Miso-shiru	Miso Soup

魚	さかな	Sakana	Fish
肉	にく	Niku	Meat
野菜	やさい	Yasai	Vegetables
デザート	でざーと	Dezaato	Dessert
卵	たまご	Tamago	Egg
焼き鳥	やきとり	Yakitori	Grilled Chicken Skewers
ラーメン	らーめん	Raamen	Ramen
カフェ	かふぇ	Kafe	Cafe
ビール	びーる	Bīru	Beer
甘い	あまい	Amai	Sweet
辛い	からい	Karai	Spicy
美味しい	おいしい	Oishii	Delicious
食べる	たべる	Taberu	To Eat
飲む	のむ	Nomu	To Drink
会計	かいけい	Kaikei	Bill (at a restaurant)

予約	よやく	Yoyaku	Reservation
お勧め	おすすめ	Osusume	Recommendation
冷たい	つめたい	Tsumetai	Cold (Temperature)
温かい	あたたかい	Atatakai	Warm (Temperature)
店員	てんいん	Tenin	Waiter/Waitress

Chapter 5 - Shopping

Shopping in Japan can be one of the best things to do when you get here! Most stores are known for their excellent customer service and attentive staff. When you walk into a Japanese shop they will great you with いらっしゃいませ (irasshaimase) which means "welcome!"

Common Shopping Phrases

Japanese	Furigana	Romaji	English
これを買いたいんですが。	これ を かいたいん です が。	Kore o kaitai n desu ga.	I would like to buy this.
値段はいくらですか。	ねだん は いくら です か。	Nedan wa ikura desu ka.	How much does it cost?
ディスカウントはありますか。	でぃすかうんと は あります か。	Disukaunto wa arimasu ka.	Is there a discount?
商品は返品できますか。	しょうひん は へんぴん できます か。	Shōhin wa henpin dekimasu ka.	Is it possible to return the item?
他におすすめのものはありますか。	ほか に おすすめ の もの は あります か。	Hoka ni osusume no mono wa arimasu ka.	Do you have any other recommendations?
これはセール品ですか。	これ は せーるひん です か。	Kore wa se-ruhin desu ka.	Is this item on sale?

これは売り切れですか。	これ は うりきれ です か。	Kore wa urikire desu ka.	Is this item sold out?

Clothing and Apparel Stores

Japanese	Furigana	Romaji	English
これはサイズが合いますか。	これ は さいず が あいます か。	Kore wa saizu ga aimasuka.	Does this come in my size?
他に色はありますか。	ほか に いろ は あります か。	Hoka ni iro wa arimasu ka.	Are there other colors available?
試着してもいいですか。	しちゃくして も いい です か。	Shichaku shite mo ii desu ka.	May I try it on?
これは新着商品ですか。	これ は しんちゃく しんぴん です か。	Kore wa shinchaku shinpin desu ka.	Is this a new arrival?
サイズが合うか確認したいです。	さいず が あう かかくにん したい です。	Saizu ga au ka kakunin shitai desu.	I want to check if the size fits.
これは人気の商品ですか。	これ は にんき の しょうひん です か。	Kore wa ninki no shouhin desu ka.	Is this a popular item?
他に同じデザインのものはありますか。	ほか に おなじ でざいん の もの は あります か。	Hoka ni onaji dezain no mono wa arimasu ka.	Do you have this in the same design?

Electronic Stores

Japanese	Furigana	Romaji	English
この製品は最新ですか。	この せいひん は さいしん です か。	Kore no seihin wa saishin desu ka.	Is this product the latest model?
この商品の特別な機能は何ですか。	この しょうひん の とくべつ な きのう は なん です か。	Kono shouhin no tokubetsu na kinou wa nan desu ka.	What are the special features of this product?
保証期間はどれくらいですか。	ほしょう きかん は どれ くらい です か。	Hoshou kikan wa dore kurai desu ka.	How long is the warranty period?
充電器は別売りですか。	じゅうでんき は べつうり です か。	Juudenki wa betsuuri desu ka.	Is the charger sold separately?
このテレビは 4K ですか。	この てれび は フォーケイですか。	Kono terebi wa foa kei desu ka.	Is this TV 4K?
ディスプレイの解像度は高いですか。	でいすぷれい の かいぞうど は たかい です か。	Disupurei no kaizoudo wa takai desu ka.	Is the display resolution high?
アフターサービスはありますか。	あふたーさーびす は あります か。	Afutā saabisu wa arimasu ka.	Is there after-sales service?
送料は無料ですか。	そうりょう は むりょう です か。	Souryou wa muryou desu ka.	Is shipping free?

操作方法を教えていただけますか。	そうさ ほうほう を おしえて いただけます か。	Sousa houhou o oshiete itadakemasu ka.	Could you show me how to operate this?
バッテリーの持続時間はどれくらいですか。	ばってりー の じぞく じかん は どれ くらい です か。	Batterii no jizoku jikan wa dore kurai desu ka.	How long does the battery last?
このカメラのズーム倍率は何倍ですか。	この かめら の ずーむ ばいそう は なんばい です か。	Kono kamera no zuumu baisou wa nanbai desu ka.	What is the zoom ratio of this camera?

Souvenirs and Gift Shopping

Omiyage is an important part of Japanese culture. Although omiyage is usually translated as "souvenir" it is much more than that. Omiyage are small gifts given to the people in your life every time you take a trip somewhere. They usually consist of small individually packed sweets that are specialty products of the place they are made. For instance, if you go to Kyoto over New Year's break, you will usually buy some matcha sweets for omiyage, as matcha is a popular product of Kyoto. You would buy some sweets for your friends and family, as well as your coworkers, so you can take them into the office to share. This means that everywhere you go in Japan, omiyage is on sale with special products and flavors from the region. These sweet or sometimes savory snacks are usually packaged individually with 5 to 30 or more snacks in one box to make them easy to distribute among your friends and coworkers.

Japanese	Furigana	Romaji	English
お土産を買いたいです。	おみやげ を かいたい です。	Omiyage o kaitai desu.	I want to buy souvenirs.

これは贈り物に適していますか。	これ は おくりもの に てきして います か。	Kore wa okurimono ni tekishiteimasu ka.	Is this suitable for a gift?
お店でラッピングしてもらえますか。	おみせ で らっぴんぐして もらえます か。	Omise de rappingu shite moraemasu ka.	Can you wrap it in the store?
これは日本らしいお土産ですね。	これ は にほん らしい おみやげ です ね。	Kore wa Nihon rashii omiyage desu ne.	This is a souvenir that seems Japanese.
友達に贈るプレゼントを探しています。	ともだち に おくる ぷれぜんと を さがして います。	Tomodachi ni okuru purezento o sagashiteimasu.	I'm looking for a gift to give to a friend.

Payment and Transactions

Japanese	Furigana	Romaji	English
クレジットカードは使えますか。	くれじっとかーど は つかえます か。	Kurejitto kaado wa tsukaemasu ka.	Can I use a credit card?
デビットカードも利用できますか。	でびっとかーど も りよう できます か。	Debitto kaado mo riyou dekimasu ka.	Can I also use a debit card?
現金で払うことはできますか。	げんきん で はらう こと は できます か。	Genkin de harau koto wa dekimasu ka.	Can I pay in cash?

クーポンは使えますか。	くーぽん は つかえます か。	Kuupon wa tsukaemasu ka.	Can I use a coupon?
割引コードを入力する方法を教えてください。	わりびきこーど を にゅうりょく する ほうほう を おしえて ください。	Waribiki koudo o nyuuryoku suru houhou o oshiete kudasai.	Please tell me how to enter a discount code.
領収書をもらえますか。	りょうしゅうしょ を もらえます か。	Ryoushuusho o moraemasu ka.	Can I have a receipt?
小銭はありますか。	こぜに は あります か。	Kozeni wa arimasu ka.	Do you have change?
クレジットカードの手数料はかかりますか。	くれじっとかーど の てすうりょう は かかります か。	Kurejitto kaado no tesuuryou wa kakarimasu ka.	Is there a fee for using a credit card?
これを持ってレジへ行きます。	これ を もって れじ へいきます。	Kore o motte reji e ikimasu.	I will take this to the checkout.
支払いはカウンターで行いますか。	しはらい は かうんたー で おこないます か。	Shiharai wa kauntaa de okonaimasuka.	Is the payment done at the counter?
チップを渡してもいいですか。	ちっぷ を わたして も いい です か。	Chippu o watashite mo ii desu ka.	Can I give a tip?
レシートをメールで送ってもらえますか。	れしーと を めーる で おくって もらえます か。	Reshiito o meeru de okutte moraemasu ka.	Can you send the receipt by email?

| お釣りはいくらで すか。 | おつり は いくら です か。 | Otsuri wa ikura desu ka. | How much is the change? |

Useful Vocabulaury for Shopping

Japanese	Furigana	Romaji	English
買い物	かいもの	Kaimono	Shopping
店	みせ	Mise	Store/Shop
売り場	うりば	Uriba	Sales Floor/Section
商品	しょうひん	Shohin	Product
価格	かかく	Kakaku	Price
割引	わりびき	Waribiki	Discount
セール	せーる	Seeru	Sale
買う	かう	Kau	To Buy
売る	うる	Uru	To Sell
現金	げんきん	Genkin	Cash
クレジットカード	くれじっとかあど	Kurejitto kaado	Credit Card

領収書	りょうしゅうしょ	Ryoushuusho	Receipt
買い物かご	かいものかご	Kaimono kago	Shopping Basket
試着室	しちゃくしつ	Shichakushitsu	Fitting Room
交換	こうかん	Koukan	Exchange
サイズ	さいず	Saizu	Size
色	いろ	Iro	Color
デザイン	でざいん	Dezain	Design
購入する	こうにゅうする	Kounyuu suru	To Purchase
バーゲン	ばあげん	Baagen	Bargain/Sale
お釣り	おつり	Otsuri	Change (money)
消費税	しょうひぜい	Shouhizei	Consumption Tax
クーポン	くうぽん	Kuupon	Coupon

Chapter 6 – Hospitals, pharmacies

If you need to go to a doctor while you are in Japan, make sure you get travel insurance before your trip. But even if you don't have insurance, you can walk into any clinic and get treated, but the price will be higher.

Japanese hospitals are usually by reference only, so seeing a regular doctor first is your best bet when you have a problem. In Japan, many small clinics specialize in areas, such as an ear, nose, and throat clinic, podiatry, or orthopedics. These clinics are free to walk in and get treated the same day.

Emergency Situations

If you are in an emergency in Japan, make sure to dial 110, which is the emergency phone number. Almost every place has a translator who will be able to speak to you in your native language. Here are some more phrases to learn in case of emergencies:

Japanese	Furigana	Romaji	English
助けてください。	たすけて ください。	Tasukete kudasai.	Please help.
110 番に電話してください。	ひゃくとおばん に でんわ して ください。	Hyaku to oban ni denwa shite kudasai.	Call 110 (emergency number).
救急車が必要です。	きゅうきゅうしゃ が ひつよう です。	Kyuukyuu sha ga hitsuyou desu.	We need an ambulance.
火事です！	かじ です！	Kaji desu!	Fire!
けがをしました。	けが を しました。	Kega o shimashita.	I am injured.

| 急いで病院に行かな けれ ばなりません。 | いそいで びょういん に いかなければ なりません。 | Isoide byouin ni ikanakereba narimasen. | I need to go to the hospital quickly. |

Medical History

If you have to go to the hospital they will surely ask you a few questions about your medical history so they can treat you. Be sure to know the Japanese words for any chronic problems you have and a list of your medications in case of an emergency.

Japanese	Furigana	Romaji	English
アレルギーがあり ます。	あれるぎー が あります。	Arerugii ga arimasu.	I have allergies.
以前に手術を受け ました。	いぜん に しゅじゅつ を うけました。	Izen ni shujutsu o ukemashita.	I had surgery before.
慢性の病気があり ます。	まんせい の びょうき が あります。	Mansei no byouki ga arimasu.	I have a chronic illness.
薬を毎日飲んでい ます。	くすり を まいにち のんで います。	Kusuri o mainichi nondeimasu.	I take medicine every day.
高血圧です。	こうけつあつ です。	Kouketsuatsu desu.	I have high blood pressure.
糖尿病になりまし た。	とうにょうびょう に なりました。	Tounyoubyou ni narimashita.	I developed diabetes.
妊娠中です。	にんしん ちゅう です。	Ninshin chuu desu.	I am pregnant.

Explaining Symptoms to a Doctor

Japanese	Furigana	Romaji	English
頭が痛いです。	あたま が いたい です。	Atama ga itai desu.	I have a headache.
喉が痛いです。	のど が いたい です。	Nodo ga itai desu.	My throat hurts.
熱があります。	ねつ が あります。	Netsu ga arimasu.	I have a fever.
寒気がします。	さむけ が します。	Samuke ga shimasu.	I feel chills.
吐き気がします。	はきけ が します。	Hakike ga shimasu.	I feel nauseous.
腹痛があります。	ふくつう が あります。	Fukutsuu ga arimasu.	I have stomach pain.
痰が絡んでいます。	たん が からんで います。	Tan ga karandeimasu.	I have phlegm.
めまいがします。	めまい が します。	Memai ga shimasu.	I feel dizzy.
全身がだるいです。	ぜんしん が だるい です。	Zenshin ga darui desu.	I feel tired all over.
傷が痛みます。	きず が いたみます。	Kizu ga itamimasu.	My wound hurts.

Medication and Dosage

In Japanese clinics, they will usually hand you a paper for your prescription. Then you will have to find a pharmacy to fill it. Thankfully you probably won't have to go far, as most clinics have pharmacies right next door or around the corner. At the pharmacy, you will have to give them your prescription and fill out a form with a few simple questions. Then they will give you your medication and you can ask the pharmacist if you have any questions.

Japanese	Furigana	Romaji	English
この薬を飲むべきですか？	この くすり を のむ べき です か？	Kono kusuri o nomu beki desu ka?	Should I take this medicine?
1日何回飲めばいいですか？	いちにち なんかい のめば いい です か？	Ichi-nichi nankai nomeba ii desu ka?	How many times should I take it in a day?
飲む前に食べるべきですか？	のむ まえ に たべる べき です か？	Nomu mae ni taberu beki desu ka?	Should I eat before taking it?
水と一緒に飲んでください。	みず と いっしょ に のんで ください。	Mizu to issho ni nonde kudasai.	Please take it with water.
この薬の副作用は何ですか？	この くすり の ふくさよう は なん です か？	Kono kusuri no fukusayou wa nan desu ka?	What are the side effects of this medicine?
忘れずに毎日同じ時間に飲んでください。	わすれず に まいにち おなじ じかん に のんで ください。	Wasurezu ni mainichi onaji jikan ni nonde kudasai.	Don't forget to take it at the same time every day.

処方箋が必要ですか？	しょほうせん が ひつよう です か？	Shohousen ga hitsuyou desu ka?	Do I need a prescription?

Making Appointments

Japanese	Furigana	Romaji	English
医者に診てもらいたいのですが。	いしゃ に みて もらいたい の です が。	Isha ni mite moraitai no desu ga.	I would like to see a doctor.
診療予約をしたいのですが。	しんりょう よやく を したい の です が。	Shinryou yoyaku o shitai no desu ga.	I would like to make a medical appointment.
病院の予約はどうすればいいですか？	びょういん の よやく は どう すれば いい です か？	Byouin no yoyaku wa dou sureba ii desu ka?	How can I make an appointment at the hospital?
緊急の場合、すぐに診てもらえますか？	きんきゅう の ばあい、すぐに みて もらえます か？	Kinkyuu no baai, sugu ni mite moraemasu ka?	In case of an emergency, can I be seen right away?
月曜日の午前中に予約がありますか？	げつようび の ごぜん ちゅう に よやく が あります か？	Getsuyoubi no gozenchuu ni yoyaku ga arimasu ka?	Do you have appointments available on Monday morning?
予約の変更は可能ですか？	よやく の へんこう は かのう です か？	Yoyaku no henkou wa kanou desu ka?	Is it possible to change the appointment?

予約をキャンセルしたいのですが。	よやく を きゃんせる したい の です が。	Yoyaku o kyanseru shitai no desu ga.	I would like to cancel the appointment.

Insurance and Payment

Japanese	Furigana	Romaji	English
診療費は保険で賄えますか？	しんりょう ひ は ほけん で まかえます か？	Shinryouhi wa hoken de mokaemasu ka?	Can I cover the medical expenses with insurance?
保険証を見せてもよろしいでしょうか？	ほけん しょう を みせて も よろしい でしょう か？	Hokenshou o misete mo yoroshii deshou ka?	May I show you my insurance card?
自己負担分はいくらですか？	じこふたん ぶん は いくら です か？	Jikofutan-bun wa ikura desu ka?	How much is the patient's share?
薬の支払いは別途ですか？	くすり の しはらい は べっと です か？	Kusuri no shiharai wa betto desu ka?	Is the payment for medicine separate?
健康保険が適用されますか？	けんこう ほけん が てきよう されます か？	Kenkou hoken ga tekiyou saremasu ka?	Is health insurance applicable?
レセプションでお支払いいただけますか？	れせぷしょん で おしはらい いただけます か？	Resepushon de oshiharai itadakemasu ka?	Can I make the payment at the reception?

Useful Vocabulary for Hospitals and Pharmacies

Japanese	Furigana	Romaji	English
病院	びょういん	Byouin	Hospital
薬局	やっきょく	Yakkyoku	Pharmacy
医者	いしゃ	Isha	Doctor
看護師	かんごし	Kangoshi	Nurse
薬	くすり	Kusuri	Medicine
処方箋	しょほうせん	Shohousen	Prescription
痛い	いたい	Itai	Painful
発熱	はつねつ	Hatsunetsu	Fever
咳	せき	Seki	Cough
喉の痛み	のどのいたみ	Nodo no itami	Sore throat
包帯	ほうたい	Houtai	Bandage
注射	ちゅうしゃ	Chuusha	Injection
副作用	ふくさよう	Fukusayou	Side effect

診察室	しんさつしつ	Shinsatsushitsu	Examination room
血圧	けつあつ	Ketsuatsu	Blood pressure
歯痛	しつう	Shitsuu	Toothache
健康保険証	けんこうほけんしょう	Kenkou hokenshou	Health insurance card
出血	しゅっけつ	Shukketsu	Bleeding
飲み薬	のみぐすり	Nomigusuri	Oral medicine

Chapter 7 - What not to do in Japan

In every country you visit, some taboos are looked down on, and Japan is no different. Before we discussed a few about bowing, and the use of chopsticks at restaurant, but below are a few more situations you might run into. If you are well prepared, you won't make any big mistakes. But if you do, just apologize, and move on, Japanese people tend to be very forgiving and friendly when others are learning about their culture.

Japanese	Furigana	Romaji	English
日本の温泉では、タトゥーを見せないでください。	にほん の おんせん では、 たとう を みせない で ください。	Nihon no onsen de wa, tatou o misenai de kudasai.	In Japanese hot springs, please don't show tattoos.
電車で大声で話さないでください。	でんしゃ で おおごえ で はなさない で ください。	Densha de oogoe de hanasanai de kudasai.	Don't speak loudly on the train.
公共の場で大声で携帯を使わないでください。	こうきょう の ば で おおごえ で けいたい を つかわない で ください。	Koukyou no ba de oogoe de keitai o tsukawanai de kudasai.	Please don't use your mobile loudly in public places.
お土産を渡すときは、両手で渡してください。	おみやげ を わたす とき は、 りょうて で わたして ください。	Omiyage o watasu toki wa, ryoute de watashite kudasai.	When giving gifts, please pass them with both hands.

食べ物を歩きながら食べないでください。	たべもの を あるき ながら たべない で ください。	Tabemono o aruki nagara tabenai de kudasai.	Please don't eat while walking.
公共の場でゴミを捨てないでください。	こうきょう の ば で ごみ を すてない で ください。	Koukyou no ba de gomi o sutenaide kudasai.	Please don't litter in public places.
日本の寺社では、靴を脱いでください。	にほん の てらしゃ では、 くつ を ぬいで ください。	Nihon no tera sha de wa, kutsu o nuide kudasai.	Inside Japanese temples and shrines, please take off your shoes.
知らない人の写真を撮らないでください。	しらないひと の しゃしん を とらない で ください。	Shiranai hito no shashin o toranai de kudasai.	Please don't take pictures of strangers.
箸で指を指さないでください。	はし で ゆび を さない で ください。	Hashi de yubi o sanaide kudasai.	Please don't point with chopsticks.
ゴミはプラスチックと可燃物を分けて捨ててください。	ごみ は ぷらすちっく と かねんぶつ を わけて すてて ください。	Gomi wa purasuchikku to kanenbutsu o wakete sutete kudasai.	Please separate plastic and burnable garbage before disposing of it.
レストランでのチップは必要ありません。	れすとらん で の ちっぷ は ひつよう ありません。	Resutoran de no chippu wa hitsuyou arimasen.	Tipping is not necessary in restaurants.

| タクシーのドアは自動で開くので、開けなくても大丈夫です。 | たくしー の どあ は じどう で ひらく ので、あけなくても だいじょうぶ です。 | Takushii no doa wa jidou de hiraku node, akenakutemo daijoubu desu. | The doors of taxis open automatically, so you don't have to open them. |

Useful Vocabulary for What Not to Do in Japan

Japanese	Furigana	Romaji	English
温泉	おんせん	Onsen	Hot Spring
タトゥー	たとう	Tatou	Tattoo
電車	でんしゃ	Densha	Train
大声	おおごえ	Oogoe	Loud Voice
話す	はなす	Hanasu	Speak
公共の場	こうきょうのば	Koukyou no ba	Public Place
携帯	けいたい	Keitai	Mobile Phone
使う	つかう	Tsukau	Use
お土産	おみやげ	Omiyage	Souvenir
渡す	わたす	Watasu	Give/Pass

両手	りょうて	Ryoute	Both Hands
食べ物	たべもの	Tabemono	Food
歩く	あるく	Aruku	Walk
公共の場	こうきょうのば	Koukyou no ba	Public Place
ゴミ	ごみ	Gomi	Garbage
捨てる	すてる	Suteru	Dispose
寺社	てらしゃ	Tera sha	Temple/Shrine
靴	くつ	Kutsu	Shoes
脱ぐ	ぬぐ	Nugu	Take off
知らない人	しらないひと	Shiranai hito	Stranger
写真	しゃしん	Shashin	Photo
取る	とる	Toru	Take
箸	はし	Hashi	Chopsticks
指さす	ゆびさす	Yubi sasu	Point with Fingers
プラスチック	ぷらすちっく	Purasuchikku	Plastic

可燃物	かねんぶつ	Kanenbutsu	Burnable Garbage
レストラン	れすとらん	Resutoran	Restaurant
チップ	ちっぷ	Chippu	Tip
必要	ひつよう	Hitsu you	Necessary
タクシー	たくしー	Takushii	Taxi
ドア	どあ	Doa	Door
自動	じどう	Jidou	Automatic

Japanese Short Stories For Language Learners:
Learn and Improve Your Japanese Comprehension Through 20 Short Stories Based Off Japan's Captivating History

Worldwide Nomad

Notice:

This book may contain:

- Interpretations of historical events.

- Cultural perspectives.

- The author's personal views on Japanese history.

Always remember that learning a language is a continuous journey. Practice, patience, and curiosity are key. Enjoy the adventure!

Yamato Period (250-710)

総武公子聖徳の説話

昔々、大和時代の日本に、総武という名の公子がいました。彼の名前は聖徳といい、他の人々よりも特別な力を持っていました。しかし、それは生まれつきのものではなく、努力と学びによって培われたものでした。

公子聖徳は、若い頃から知識を渇望し、多くの学者から学びました。彼はまた、人々との関わりを大切にし、彼の知識と理解力を用いて、人々の生活を改善しました。

ある日、聖徳の国に大きな飢饉が訪れました。聖徳は、この機会に国を助けることで、更にその力を拡大することを決意しました。彼は最も賢い農夫と一緒に、飢饉に耐えうる作物を栽培する方法を考えました

飢饉が続く中、聖徳と農夫たちは、人々が飢えを凌ぐことができるように、夜を徹して作物を栽培しました。数日後、作物は豊かに実り、人々は飢饉から回復し始めました。人々は聖徳の恩義に深く感謝し、彼の力はさらに強大となりました。

この出来事がきっかけとなり、聖徳の治世は全国に広がりました。聖徳は、自分の力が最も力強い存在となったことを誇りに思いました。しかし、その力を持続するためには、賢明に行動する必要がありました。

年月が経ち、聖徳は年老いていきましたが、彼の知恵と策略は次代へと受け継がれました。聖徳の名は、その後も長きにわたり、日本の地で最も尊敬される名として語り継がれました。

The Tale of Prince Shotoku of Yamato

Once upon a time, in the Yamato period of Japan, there was a prince named Sōmu. His given name was Shotoku, and he possessed a special power beyond that of ordinary people. However, it wasn't something he was born with, but something he cultivated through hard work and learning.

From a young age, Prince Shotoku thirsted for knowledge and learned from many scholars. He also valued interactions with people, using his knowledge and understanding to improve their lives.

One day, a great famine struck Shotoku's kingdom. Shotoku saw this as an opportunity to assist his country and further expand his influence. He collaborated with the wisest farmers to devise ways to cultivate crops that could withstand the famine.

As the famine persisted, Shotoku and the farmers worked tirelessly through the night to cultivate crops that could help people stave off hunger. A few days later, the crops flourished, and the people began to recover from the famine. They deeply appreciated Shotoku's benevolence, and his power grew even stronger.

This incident led to the expansion of Shotoku's reign throughout the country. Shotoku was proud that his power became the most potent entity. However, to sustain this power, he needed to act wisely.

As the years passed, even though Shotoku grew old, his wisdom and strategies were passed down to subsequent generations. The name of Shotoku continued to be revered as one of the most respected names in Japan for a long time.

Vocabulary

- 公子 (Kōshi) - Prince

- 知識 (Chishiki) - Knowledge

- 飢饉 (Kikin) - Famine

- 栽培 (Saibai) - Cultivate

- 恩義 (On'gi) - Gratitude

Comprehension Questions:

聖徳公子が何をして力を増大させたのか？ What did Prince Shotoku do to increase his power?

聖徳公子はどのようにして飢饉の国を救いましたか？ How did Prince Shotoku save the country from famine?

なぜ聖徳公子は他の人々よりも強力であったのですか？ Why was Prince Shotoku more powerful than others?

Heian Period(794-1185)

平安時代の初期武士の登場

昔々、平安時代の日本に、武士と呼ばれる新たな階級が現れました。この階級は、皇室や貴族から離れて、自分たちだけの世界を作り出しました。その中でも、最初の武士たちは、力と名誉を求めて戦い、土地を守り、法を守るために力を使いました。

ある日、彼らの中から一人の男が立ち上がりました。彼の名前は源頼朝、新たな時代を切り開くための道を開く者でした。彼は、自らの力と信念を持って、武士たちを統一し、新たな秩序を築くことを決意しました。

源頼朝は、普段の平穏な日々に変化を求めていました。彼は、自分の力と知識を使って、新たな政治体制を作り出すことを決意しました。そのために、彼は自分の周りの武士たちを集め、共に戦うことを誓いました。

彼の行動は、他の武士たちからも支持を受けました。彼らは、源頼朝の強い意志と、新たな秩序を作り出すための彼の計画に感銘を受けました。そして、彼らは一緒になって、新たな時代を作り出すために戦い始めました。

源頼朝のリーダーシップの下、彼らは数々の戦いを経験しました。しかし、彼らは常に団結し、共に前進し続けました。その結果、新たな時代が幕を開けました。これが、日本の武士たちの時代の始まりでした。

そして、源頼朝は、新たな時代のリーダーとして、武士たちに尊敬と信頼を得ることができました。彼は、自分の力と知恵を使って、新たな秩序を作り出し、武士たちの生活を向上させることができました。

しかし、源頼朝は、自分の力と地位を維持するためには、常に警戒心を持ち続ける必要があることを理解していました。彼は、自分の力と地位を維持し続けるために、常に新たな戦略を考え出し、自分の力を試し続けました。

そして、源頼朝の時代が終わったとき、彼の精神と戦略は次の世代に引き継がれました。そして、武士たちは、その後の数世紀にわたり、日本の政治と社会に大きな影響を与え続けました。

これが、日本の武士たち、そして彼らの時代の始まりの物語です。彼らは、自分たちの力と知識を使って、新たな時代を作り出し、自分たちの生活を向上させることができました。

The Emergence of the Early Samurai in the Heian Period

Once upon a time, in the Heian period of Japan, a new class known as samurai emerged. This class distanced themselves from the imperial family and nobility, creating a world of their own. The first samurai used their strength to fight for power and honor, protect their land, and enforce the law.

One day, a man stood out among them. His name was Minamoto no Yoritomo, the one who paved the way for a new era. He decided to unify the samurai with his strength and conviction and establish a new order.

Minamoto no Yoritomo desired a change from the usual peaceful days. He decided to use his strength and knowledge to establish a new political system. To do this, he gathered the samurai around him and vowed to fight together.

His actions were supported by other samurai. They were impressed by Yoritomo's strong will and his plan to create a new order. Together, they began to fight to create a new era.

Under Yoritomo's leadership, they experienced many battles. However, they always stuck together and continued to move forward. As a result, a new era dawned. This was the beginning of the era of the samurai in Japan.

And so, Yoritomo, as the leader of the new era, earned the respect and trust of the samurai. He was able to improve the lives of the samurai by creating a new order with his strength and wisdom.

However, Yoritomo understood that he needed to always be vigilant to maintain his power and position. He constantly devised new strategies and tested his strength to maintain his power and position.

And when Yoritomo's era ended, his spirit and strategies were passed on to the next generation. And the samurai continued to have a significant impact on Japanese politics and society for centuries to follow.

This is the story of the beginning of the samurai in Japan, and their era. They were able to create a new era, and improve their lives, using their strength and knowledge.

Vocabulary

- 武士 (Bushi) - Samurai

- 源頼朝 (Minamoto no Yoritomo) - Minamoto no Yoritomo

- 階級 (Kaikyū) - Class

- 時代 (Jidai) - Era

- 土地 (Tochi) - Land

Comprehension Questions:

初期の武士たちは何を求めて戦いましたか？ What did the early samurai fight for?

源頼朝は何を目指していましたか？ What did Minamoto no Yoritomo aim to do?

源頼朝の行動はどのように他の武士たちに影響を与えましたか？ How did Minamoto no Yoritomo's actions influence other samurai?

源平合戦の物語

昔々、日本の平安時代に、源氏と平家という二つの名家がありました。源氏は勇猛な武将を多く輩出し、平家は皇族と親しい関係を持つことで知られていました。両家は力を競い合い、時には争いを起こすこともありました。

ある日、皇位を巡る争いが起こりました。源氏は自分たちの立場を強めるために、争いに介入することを決めました。しかし、平家は皇族とのつながりを利用して、皇位を手中に収めようと画策しました。

源氏の一部は、平家の計画を阻止するために、秘密裏に行動を開始しました。彼らは夜陰に紛れて平家の本陣を襲撃し、皇位を巡る闘いに一石を投じました。しかし、平家もまた、その動きに対抗するための策略を練り始めました。

多くの戦闘が行われ、両家は数多くの勇士を失いました。しかし、源氏は勇猛さと知恵を活かし、徐々に優勢に立ち始めました。一方、平家は皇族とのつながりを活かして、なおも抵抗を続けました。

この争いは結果的に、源氏が平家を破る形で終わりました。しかし、その勝利は犠牲と引き換えに得られたもので、源氏の一部はその代償を痛感しました。源氏の勝利は、後の時代に影響を与え、日本の歴史を形成する一端を担いました。

平安時代は、源氏と平家の争いを通じて、その終焉を迎えました。しかし、その時代の物語は、日本の歴史と文化の中に深く刻まれ、今日まで語り継がれています。そして、その物語は、我々が学ぶべき教訓と共に、未来へと繋がっています。

The Tale of the Genpei War

Once upon a time, during the Heian period in Japan, there were two prominent families, the Minamoto and the Taira, known as Genji and Heike, respectively. The Genji were known for producing brave warriors, and the Heike were known for their close relations with the royal family. Both families competed for power, sometimes leading to conflicts.

One day, a dispute arose over the imperial succession. The Genji decided to intervene in the dispute to strengthen their position. However, the Heike plotted to take control of the throne using their connections with the royal family.

Some of the Genji began to act secretly to thwart the Heike's plans. They attacked the Heike's headquarters under cover of darkness, throwing a wrench into the fight for the throne. However, the Heike also began to devise strategies to counter this move.

Many battles were fought, and both families lost many brave warriors. However, the Genji, using their valor and wisdom, gradually began to gain the upper hand. Meanwhile, the Heike continued to resist, leveraging their connections with the royal family.

The conflict eventually ended with the Genji defeating the Heike. However, this victory was obtained at the expense of many sacrifices, and some of the Genji deeply felt the cost. The victory of the Genji influenced later eras and played a part in shaping the history of Japan.

The Heian period came to an end through the conflict between the Genji and the Heike. However, the stories of that era are deeply engraved in Japanese history and culture and continue to be passed down to this day. And these stories connect to the future, along with the lessons we should learn.

Vocabulary

- 源氏 (Genji) - Minamoto clan

- 平家 (Heike) - Taira clan

- 皇位 (Kōi) - Imperial throne

- 争い (Arasoi) - Conflict

- 勇士 (Yūshi) - Brave warrior

- 勝利 (Shōri) - Victory

Comprehension Questions

源氏と平家が争ったのは何のためですか？ What was the conflict between the Genji and the Heike about?

源氏はどのようにして闘いに勝つことができましたか？ How were the Genji able to win the fight?

平家の力はどこから来ていましたか？ Where did the power of the Heike come from?

Kamakura Period (1185-1333)

モンゴルの日本侵攻

かつて、日本の鎌倉時代に、名も無き侍がいました。この侍は、敵も味方も認めるほどの剣の達人で、その技には誰も敵わないとされていました。彼の名前は知られていませんでしたが、その勇敢さと剣術の腕前は、多くの人々を惹きつけました。

しかし、ある日、遥かなる大陸より、モンゴルの大軍が日本に侵攻しました。彼らの数は圧倒的で、侍たちの間に恐怖が広がりました。しかし、名も無き侍は他の侍たちを鼓舞し、彼らと共に戦うことを決意しました。

侍たちは、モンゴル軍の前に立ちはだかりました。名も無き侍は剣を振るい、一人でも多くの敵を討つことを誓いました。彼の戦いぶりは、周りの侍たちに勇気を与え、彼らもまた、敵に立ち向かう決意を新たにしました。

しかし、モンゴル軍の圧力は強く、侍たちは次々と倒れていきました。名も無き侍もまた、深い傷を負い、ついには倒れてしまいました。しかし、彼の戦いぶりは、侍たちの間で語り継がれ、彼らの心に火をつけました。

侍たちは、名も無き侍の勇敢さに触発され、再び立ち上がりました。モンゴル軍に立ち向かう彼らの中には、名も無き侍の勇敢さを忘れる者はいませんでした。彼らは一致団結し、ついにはモンゴル軍を撃退することに成功しました。

しかし、その戦いでの犠牲は、語り継がれるべきものでした。名も無き侍の勇敢さは、後の世にまで語り継がれ、その名も無き英雄の物語は、多くの人々に希望と勇気を与え続けました。

彼の物語は、日本の歴史の中で、一つの重要な時期を象徴するものでした。それは、侍の勇敢さと忠誠心が、モンゴルの侵攻に対抗する力を持っていたことを示していました。

そして、その名も無き侍の物語は、日本の心を形成する一部となり、多くの人々がその精神を継承しました。彼の物語は、日本の歴史の一部として、今日まで語り継がれています。

Mongols Attack Japan

Once in the Kamakura period of Japan, there lived an anonymous samurai. This samurai was a master of the sword, recognized by friends and foes alike, and his skill was said to be unmatched. Though his name was unknown, his bravery and swordsmanship captivated many.

However, one day, a massive Mongol army invaded Japan from a distant continent. Their overwhelming numbers spread fear among the samurai, but the anonymous samurai inspired his fellow samurai and decided to fight alongside them.

The samurai stood against the Mongol army. The anonymous samurai swung his sword, vowing to slay as many enemies as possible. His fighting spirit gave courage to the surrounding samurai, and they too renewed their determination to confront the enemy.

However, the pressure of the Mongol army was strong, and one by one, the samurai fell. The anonymous samurai, too, suffered deep wounds and finally fell. However, his battle was passed down among the samurai, kindling a fire in their hearts.

Inspired by the bravery of the anonymous samurai, the samurai rose again. Among those who stood against the Mongol army, there was no one who forgot the bravery of the anonymous samurai. They united and finally succeeded in repelling the Mongol army.

However, the sacrifices made in the battle were worth telling. The bravery of the anonymous samurai was passed down to later generations, and the tale of this unnamed hero continued to give hope and courage to many.

His story symbolized a significant period in Japanese history. It showed that the bravery and loyalty of the samurai had the power to resist the Mongol invasion.

And the story of the anonymous samurai became part of the formation of the Japanese spirit, and many people inherited its spirit. His story is still being told as part of Japanese history today.

Vocabulary

- Samurai (侍) - Samurai

- Sword (剣) - Sword

- Brave (勇敢) - Brave

- Battle (戦い) - Battle

- Hero (英雄) - Hero

Comprehension Questions

名も無き侍は何故モンゴルに立ち向かったのでしょうか？ Why did the nameless samurai stand against the Mongols?

名も無き侍の遺産は何でしょうか？ What is the legacy of the nameless samurai?

この物語が日本の歴史にどのような影響を与えたのでしょうか？ How has this story influenced Japanese history?

Ashikaga Period(1336-1568)

足利時代の戦乱（1336 年-1568 年）

ある時、日本の戦国時代に、川崎という名の武将がいました。彼は他の多くの武将たちと同じく、その領地と名誉を守るために戦っていました。川崎は智に富む武将で、その統率力と戦略により、彼の領地は常に安定していました。

しかし、ある日、彼の平穏な日々は突如として終わりを告げました。隣の領地を治める武将、山城が川崎の領地を侵略しようと、大軍を派遣してきました。川崎は戦いを避けることを選び、自分の領地から撤退しました。

しかし、山城はその後も川崎の領地を追い求め、戦争は避けられない状況となりました。川崎は最終的には、自身の領地と名誉のために、戦うことを決めました。彼は自分の兵士たちを集め、山城の大軍に立ち向かう覚悟を決めました。

戦いの日、川崎は自分の兵士たちに対して、彼らの命を守るために最善を尽くすことを誓いました。そして、彼は山城の大軍に立ち向かい、戦いは始まりました。戦闘は激しく、多くの兵士が命を落としました。

しかし、川崎は自分の策略と勇気により、山城の大軍を撃退することに成功しました。彼の兵士たちは彼の名を称え、川崎の名誉は更に高まりました。この戦いは、川崎が領地を守るために、どれだけ遠くまで行くかを示すものでした。

さらに、この戦いは他の領地の武将たちにも影響を与えました。彼らは川崎の勇気と戦略の素晴らしさを認め、彼を尊敬するようになりました。これにより、川崎は他の武将たちとの同盟を結ぶことができ、彼の領地はさらに安定しました。

年月が経つにつれて、川崎の領地はさらに広がりを見せました。彼は自分の知恵と統率力により、領地の安定と繁栄を保つことができました。川崎の名は日本全国に広まり、彼はその時代最強の武将として知られるようになりました。

この物語は、戦国時代の日本の武将たちがどのようにして自分の領地と名誉を守り、またどのようにして力を増すかを示すものです。そして、それはまた、彼らがどれだけ遠くまで行くことができるかを示すものでもあります。

War and Turmoil in the Ashikaga Period (1336-1568)

Once upon a time, during the Sengoku period in Japan, there was a warlord named Kawasaki. Like many other warlords, he was fighting to protect his territory and honor. Kawasaki was a wise general, and thanks to his leadership and strategy, his territory was always stable.

However, his peaceful days came to an abrupt end one day. A warlord named Yamashiro, who ruled the neighboring territory, sent a large army to invade Kawasaki's territory. Kawasaki chose to avoid conflict and retreated from his territory.

However, Yamashiro continued to pursue Kawasaki's territory, and war became inevitable. Kawasaki ultimately decided to fight for his territory and honor. He gathered his soldiers and prepared to confront Yamashiro's large army.

On the day of the battle, Kawasaki vowed to do his best to protect the lives of his soldiers. Then, he stood against Yamashiro's large army, and the battle began. The fighting was fierce, and many soldiers lost their lives.

However, Kawasaki managed to repel Yamashiro's large army with his strategy and bravery. His soldiers hailed his name, and Kawasaki's honor grew even more. This battle showed how far Kawasaki would go to protect his territory.

Furthermore, this battle influenced the warlords of other territories. They acknowledged the greatness of Kawasaki's courage and strategy, and they began to respect him. As a result, Kawasaki was able to form alliances with other warlords, and his territory became even more stable.

As time went by, Kawasaki's territory expanded further. He was able to maintain the stability and prosperity of his territory with his wisdom and leadership. Kawasaki's name spread throughout Japan, and he became known as the strongest warlord of his time.

This tale exemplifies how warlords in Sengoku-era Japan protected their territories and honor and increased their power. It also shows how far they were willing to go.

Vocabulary

- 戦国時代 (Sengoku jidai) - Period of Warring States

- 武将 (Bushō) - Warlord

- 領地 (Ryōchi) - Territory

- 名誉 (Meiyo) - Honor

- 策略 (Sakuryaku) - Strategy

- 大軍 (Taigun) - Large army

Comprehension Questions

川崎はどのようにして自分の領地を守りましたか？ How did Kawasaki protect his territory?

川崎の戦略と勇気は何を示していますか？ What do Kawasaki's strategy and courage demonstrate?

他の武将たちが川崎を尊敬するようになった理由は何ですか？ Why did the other warlords start to respect Kawasaki?

物語一：初めてのヨーロッパ人

かつて、室町時代と呼ばれる時がありました。日本の文化と技術が大いに発展し、さまざまな芸術が栄え、新たな一族が台頭してきました。その中には足利一族という、日本の歴史において重要な役割を果たす一族がありました。

ある日、遠く異国の地から、見たこともないような船がやってきました。その船に乗っていたのは、ヨーロッパから来た初めての訪問者たちでした。彼らは日本の人々に新たな文化や技術を紹介し、日本とヨーロッパ間の交流を始めました。

足利一族の頭領は、これを大きなチャンスと捉えました。彼はヨーロッパ人たちを歓迎し、彼らの文化や技術に学びを求めました。その結果、足利一族の頭領は、他の一族よりも先進的な知識を持つことができました。

ヨーロッパ人たちは、日本の文化や習慣に大いに興味を持ちました。彼らは日本の技術や芸術、そして人々の暮らしを学び、ヨーロッパにもそれを広めました。その結果、日本とヨーロッパの間には深いつながりが生まれました。

足利一族の頭領は、この新たな関係を維持するために、ヨーロッパ人たちとの交流を続けました。彼はヨーロッパの技術や知識を日本に取り入れ、その発展に貢献しました。その結果、足利一族の影響力はさらに強まり、その名声は日本全土に広がりました。

しかし、新たな文化との接触は、日本の社会にも変化をもたらしました。ヨーロッパ人たちの持ってきた新たな考え方や技術は、日本人たちの生活を根本から変えました。それは、新たな時代の始まりを告げるものでした。

ヨーロッパ人たちとの交流は、文化的な交流だけでなく、商品の交換も行われました。ヨーロッパからは銃や硝石、そして新たな航海技術がもたらされ、日本からは金や銀、そして美しい芸術作品が送られました。

足利一族は、この新たな交流を通じて、日本の地位を高めることができました。彼らは、ヨーロッパとの交流を通じて日本の発展を促進し、新たな時代を迎える準備を始めました。

そして、足利一族の頭領は、ヨーロッパ人たちとの交流を通じて、新たな知識と視野を得ることができました。彼は、新たな技術や知識を活用して、日本の発展に貢献しました。

最後に、足利一族は、ヨーロッパ人たちとの交流を通じて、日本の未来に影響を与えることができました。彼らは、新たな文化や技術を受け入れ、日本の社会を形成するのに大きな役割を果たしました。

Story One: The First Europeans

There was once a time known as the Muromachi period. During this time, Japanese culture and technology flourished, various arts prospered, and new clans emerged. Among them was the Ashikaga clan, a family that played a significant role in Japanese history.

One day, a ship like no other arrived from a distant foreign land. Aboard the ship were the first visitors from Europe. They introduced new cultures and technologies to the Japanese people and initiated interactions between Japan and Europe.

The leader of the Ashikaga clan saw this as a significant opportunity. He welcomed the Europeans and sought to learn from their culture and technology. As a result, the leader of the Ashikaga clan was able to gain advanced knowledge ahead of other clans.

The Europeans were deeply interested in Japanese culture and customs. They learned about Japanese technology, arts, and people's lives and spread them in Europe. As a result, a deep connection was formed between Japan and Europe.

The leader of the Ashikaga clan continued to interact with the Europeans to maintain this new relationship. He incorporated European technology and knowledge into Japan and contributed to its development. As a result, the influence of the Ashikaga clan grew stronger, and their fame spread throughout Japan.

However, contact with a new culture brought changes to Japanese society. The new ideas and technologies brought by the Europeans fundamentally changed the lives of the Japanese people. It signaled the beginning of a new era.

Interaction with the Europeans involved not only cultural exchanges but also the exchange of goods. Guns, saltpeter, and new navigation technology were brought from Europe, and gold, silver, and beautiful artworks were sent from Japan.

Through this new interaction, the Ashikaga clan was able to elevate Japan's status. They promoted Japan's development through interaction with Europe and began preparations for a new era.

And finally, the leader of the Ashikaga clan was able to gain new knowledge and perspective through interaction with the Europeans. He contributed to Japan's development by utilizing new technology and knowledge.

In the end, the Ashikaga clan was able to influence Japan's future through interaction with the Europeans. They played a significant role in shaping Japanese society by accepting new cultures and technologies.

Vocabulary

- 室町時代 (Muromachi jidai) - Muromachi period

- 足利一族 (Ashikaga ichizoku) - Ashikaga clan

- ヨーロッパ (Yōroppa) - Europe

- 文化 (Bunka) - Culture

- 技術 (Gijutsu) - Technology

Comprehension Questions

ヨーロッパ人たちが日本にもたらした新たなものは何ですか？ What new things did the Europeans bring to Japan?

足利一族の頭領はどのようにヨーロッパ人たちと交流しましたか？ How did the leader of the Ashikaga clan interact with the Europeans?

ヨーロッパ人たちとの交流が日本にどのような影響を与えましたか？ What impact did the interaction with the Europeans have on Japan?

Tokugawa Period(1603-1868)

徳川時代の平和な生活

昔々、徳川時代の日本に、佐藤という名前の家族が住んでいました。彼らは農業に従事し、豊かな稲作地を所有していました。家族の主、佐藤の父は、一日中畑で働くことにより、家族を養っていました。

この時代は、日本の平和な時代であり、町の人々は日々の生活に没頭していました。佐藤家も例外ではなく、父は農作業に、母は家事に、子どもたちは学校に勤しんでいました。

ある日、佐藤家の息子が、学校から帰ってきたときに、町の中心部で見かけた商人の話を始めました。商人は外国の品物を販売しており、その中には珍しい本や芸術品も含まれていました。息子はその話を聞きながら、心の中で新しくて刺激的な世界に興奮していました。

その夜、家族が晩餐をとりながら、息子は父に商人の話をした。父は、新しいものへの好奇心を押さえつけ、息子に田舎の生活の素晴らしさを教えようとしました。しかし、息子の心はすでに新しい冒険に向けて飛び立っていました。

数年後、息子は村を離れ、未知の世界を探求する旅に出ました。家族は彼を見送り、彼が新しい世界で成功を収め、平和な生活を送ることを願っていました。

息子が旅立ってから何年も経ったある日、村に一通の手紙が届きました。手紙は息子からで、彼が都市で成功を収め、商人としての地位を築いたことを伝えていました。家族は息子の成功を祝い、村の人々もそのニュースを喜びました。

この話は、徳川時代の日本の平和な生活と、新しい可能性を追求する勇気について教えてくれます。佐藤家の息子は、自分の夢を追求する勇気を持ち、それが現実になるように努力しました。彼の物語は、夢を追求し、新しい可能性を探求することの重要性を私たちに教えてくれます。

A Peaceful Life in the Tokugawa Period

Once upon a time, in Japan during the Tokugawa period, there lived a family named Sato. They were engaged in agriculture and owned a fertile rice field. The head of the family, Sato's father, supported his family by working in the fields all day long.

This was a peaceful era in Japan, and the townspeople were immersed in their daily lives. The Sato family was no exception, with the father engaged in farming, the mother in household chores, and the children committed to school.

One day, Sato's son started telling a story about a merchant he saw in the center of town on his way home from school. The merchant was selling foreign goods, including rare books and works of art. As he listened to the story, the son was excited about the new and stimulating world in his heart.

That night, as the family had dinner, the son told his father about the merchant. The father tried to suppress his curiosity about new things and teach his son the wonderfulness of rural life. However, the son's heart had already taken off towards a new adventure.

Several years later, the son left the village and set out on a journey to explore the unknown world. The family saw him off, hoping that he would find success in the new world and lead a peaceful life.

Several years after the son left, a letter arrived in the village one day. The letter was from the son, telling that he had made a success in the city and built a position as a merchant. The family celebrated the son's success, and the villagers were also delighted with the news.

This story teaches us about the peaceful life in Japan during the Tokugawa era and the courage to pursue new possibilities. Sato's son had the courage to pursue his dream and worked to make it a reality. His story teaches us the importance of pursuing dreams and exploring new possibilities.

Vocabulary

- 農業 (Nōgyō) - Agriculture

- 商人 (Shōnin) - Merchant

- 冒険 (Bōken) - Adventure

- 夢 (Yume) - Dream

- 可能性 (Kanōsei) - Possibility

Comprehension Questions

佐藤家の息子は何に興奮していましたか？ What was Sato's son excited about?

佐藤家の息子が旅に出た理由は何でしたか？ Why did Sato's son leave on a journey?

佐藤家の息子の成功についてどのように感じましたか？ How did you feel about Sato's son's success?

徳川時代の孤独な船乗り

かつて、徳川時代の日本に、孤独な船乗りがいました。彼の名前は杉浦という。杉浦は他の多くの日本人とは違い、海に対する深い愛情を抱いていました。しかし、政府の鎖国政策により、彼は海外への航海を禁じられていました。

杉浦は毎日海を見つめ、遠い地方への憧れを抱きつつ、航海の夢を捨てることができませんでした。彼は小船をこっそり作り始め、密かに外国への航海を計画しました。

ある夜、杉浦は船に乗り、海へと漕ぎ出しました。彼の目指す地は、聞きしに勝ると言われている神秘的な外国、中国でした。彼の航海は危険で長く、孤独でしたが、彼は自分の目的を達成するためには何もかもを捧げる覚悟でした。

数ヶ月後、杉浦はついに中国に到着しました。彼はその地の人々、文化、技術に深く感動しました。しかし、彼は日本へ戻らなければならず、貴重な知識と経験を胸に秘めて航海を再開しました。

帰国後、杉浦は密かに航海の経験と中国の知識を伝え始めました。彼の話は広まり、多くの人々が海外への興味を持つきっかけとなりました。しかし、このことが政府の耳に入り、杉浦は逮捕されてしまいました。

杉浦は投獄されましたが、彼の話は引き続き広まり、人々の心を動かしました。多くの人々が海外への航海を夢見るようになり、徳川時代の閉じた世界に新たな風を吹き込みました。

杉浦の話は今でも語り継がれています。彼の冒険心と勇敢さは、国を開くきっかけとなり、日本の歴史に大きな影響を与えました。

The Lonely Sailor of the Tokugawa Period

Once upon a time, during the Tokugawa period in Japan, there lived a lonely sailor named Sugiura. Unlike many other Japanese people of his time, Sugiura had a deep love for the sea. However, due to the government's isolationist policy, he was forbidden to sail overseas.

Every day, Sugiura gazed out at the sea, yearning for far-off lands, and could not give up his dream of sailing. He began to secretly build a small boat and planned a clandestine voyage to a foreign land.

One night, Sugiura boarded his boat and rowed out to sea. His destination was the mysterious foreign land of China, said to be beyond anything he could imagine. His voyage was dangerous, long, and lonely, but he was prepared to give everything to achieve his goal.

Months later, Sugiura finally arrived in China. He was deeply moved by the people, culture, and technology of the land. However, he had to return to Japan, and he resumed his voyage, cherishing the valuable knowledge and experiences he had gained.

Upon returning home, Sugiura began to secretly share his experiences of sailing and the knowledge of China. His stories spread, sparking interest in overseas travel among many people. However, his actions came to the attention of the government, and Sugiura was arrested.

Sugiura was imprisoned, but his stories continued to spread and touched people's hearts. Many people started to dream of sailing overseas, bringing a fresh wind into the closed world of the Tokugawa era.

Sugiura's story is still passed down to this day. His adventurous spirit and bravery became a catalyst to open up the country and had a significant influence on Japan's history.

Vocabulary

- 船乗り (Funanori) - Sailor

- 鎖国政策 (Sakoku Seisaku) - Isolationist policy

- 航海 (Kōkai) - Voyage

- 中国 (Chūgoku) - China

- 投獄 (Tōgoku) - Imprisonment

Comprehension Questions

杉浦が海外へ航海する理由は何でしたか？ What was the reason Sugiura sailed overseas?

杉浦が中国から持ち帰ったものは何でしたか？ What did Sugiura bring back from China?

杉浦の話が日本人にどのような影響を与えましたか？ How did Sugiura's stories affect the Japanese people?

徳川時代のキリスト教の弾圧と外国人追放

昔々、日本には徳川という名の将軍がいました。彼は国の統一と平和を守るため、キリスト教徒とヨーロッパ人宣教師を国から追放しました。彼の政策は厳しく、外国との交易もオランダと中国だけに限定されました。

ある日、キリスト教徒の村が彼の目に留まりました。彼はその村を訪れ、キリスト教徒たちに自分の信仰を捨てるよう命じました。しかし、村人たちは信仰を捨てることを拒否しました。

将軍は彼らの反抗に怒り、村全体を焼き払う命令を出しました。しかし、村人たちの信仰は揺るがず、彼らは火の中で祈りを捧げ続けました。

その後、将軍は更に厳しい政策を施行し、キリスト教徒を発見次第、すぐに処刑するようにしました。しかし、キリスト教徒たちは密かに信仰を守り続け、地下教会を形成しました。

時が経つにつれ、将軍の政策は徐々に力を失い、キリスト教徒たちは地下から出て来て信仰を表明するようになりました。この時、日本全国には数百の地下教会が存在していました。

将軍はこれを知り、再びキリスト教徒を追放するよう命じました。しかし、彼らの信仰は揺るぎなく、再び地下に潜り、信仰を守り続けました。

このように、徳川時代の日本は、キリスト教の弾圧と外国人の追放によって、長い間孤立していました。しかし、キリスト教徒たちは決して諦めず、自分たちの信仰を守り続けました。

この物語は、どんな困難にも立ち向かい、自分の信仰を守ることの重要性を教えてくれます。そして、それは今日の日本にも通じるメッセージであり、我々が自分の信念を大切にし、それを守るべきであることを示しています。

The Suppression of Christianity and Expulsion of Foreigners in the Tokugawa Period

Once upon a time, in Japan, there was a shogun named Tokugawa. He expelled Christians and European missionaries from the country to protect the unity and peace of his nation. His policies were strict, limiting foreign trade to only the Dutch and Chinese.

One day, a Christian village caught his eye. He visited the village and commanded the Christians to renounce their faith. However, the villagers refused to abandon their beliefs.

Angered by their defiance, the shogun ordered the entire village to be burned. However, the villagers' faith did not waver, and they continued to pray amid the flames.

The shogun then implemented even stricter policies, executing Christians as soon as they were discovered. However, the Christians continued to secretly maintain their faith, forming underground churches.

As time passed, the shogun's policies gradually lost their power, and Christians began to openly declare their faith. At this time, there were hundreds of underground churches throughout Japan.

The shogun learned of this and ordered the expulsion of Christians once again. However, their faith was unwavering, and they once again went underground to maintain their faith.

In this way, Japan during the Tokugawa period was isolated for a long time due to the suppression of Christianity and the expulsion of foreigners. However, the Christians never gave up and continued to protect their faith.

This story teaches us the importance of standing up to difficulties and preserving one's faith. And it is a message that resonates with Japan today, showing us that we should cherish our beliefs and protect them.

Vocabulary

- 将軍 (Shōgun) - Shogun

- キリスト教徒 (Kirisutokyōto) - Christian

- 宣教師 (Senkyōshi) - Missionary

- 地下教会 (Chika kyōkai) - Underground church

- 信仰 (Shinkō) - Faith

Comprehension Questions

徳川将軍はなぜキリスト教徒を追放したのですか？ Why did the shogun Tokugawa expel the Christians?

キリスト教徒はどのようにして自分たちの信仰を守りましたか？ How did the Christians protect their faith?

徳川時代の日本はどのように外国との交流を制限しましたか？ How did Japan during the Tokugawa period limit its interaction with foreign countries?

浮世絵の誕生と庶民の喜び

かつて、江戸時代の日本に、庶民の間で流行の芸術がありました。それは浮世絵と呼ばれ、日常の風景や人々の生活を描いたものでした。この芸術は、庶民の間で非常に人気があり、彼らの生活を豊かにしていました。

この時代には、浮世絵師として名を馳せた二人の画家がいました。一人は葛飾北斎、もう一人は歌川広重です。彼らは、それぞれの視点から日本の美しさを描き出し、庶民の間で絶大な人気を博しました。

葛飾北斎は、特に自然の美しさを描くことで知られていました。彼の作品は、日本の風景の美しさを世界に広め、多くの人々を魅了しました。一方、歌川広重は、都市の風景や人々の生活を描くことで知られていました。

ある日、葛飾北斎は大きな画布に向かって座っていました。彼は、山や川、花や鳥などを描くことで、自然の美しさを表現しようとしました。彼の作品は、その細部まで丁寧に描かれ、観る者の心を捉える力がありました。

一方、歌川広重は、都市の風景や人々の生活を描くことを楽しんでいました。彼の作品は、都市の喧騒や人々の日常生活を描くことで、観る者にとっての喜びをもたらしていました。

こうして、彼らの作品は庶民の間で非常に人気があり、多くの人々が彼らの作品を楽しむために、浮世絵を買い求めました。また、彼らの作品は、庶民が日常生活の中で美を見つける手助けをしました。

これらの画家たちの作品は、現代のマンガやアニメの原型となり、日本の芸術と文化を世界に広める役割を果たしました。彼らの作品は、庶民が生活の中で美を見つけることの大切さを教えてくれる貴重な宝物でした。

葛飾北斎と歌川広重の作品は、今日でも多くの人々に愛されています。彼らの作品は、日本の芸術と文化の素晴らしさを伝えるための重要な一部となっています。

The Birth of Ukiyo-e and the Joy of the Common People

Once upon a time, during the Edo period in Japan, there was a popular art form among the common people. It was called ukiyo-e, and it depicted everyday landscapes and people's lives. This art form was very popular among the common people and enriched their lives.

There were two painters who made a name for themselves as ukiyo-e artists during this time. One was Katsushika Hokusai, and the other was Utagawa Hiroshige. They each depicted the beauty of Japan from their perspectives and gained immense popularity among the common people.

Katsushika Hokusai was particularly known for depicting the beauty of nature. His works spread the beauty of Japanese landscapes to the world and captivated many people. On the other hand, Utagawa Hiroshige was known for depicting urban landscapes and people's lives.

One day, Katsushika Hokusai sat in front of a large canvas. He tried to express the beauty of nature by drawing mountains, rivers, flowers, and birds. His works, carefully drawn down to the details, had the power to capture the viewer's heart.

Meanwhile, Utagawa Hiroshige enjoyed depicting urban landscapes and people's lives. His works brought joy to the viewers by depicting the hustle and bustle of the city and people's daily lives.

Thus, their works were very popular among the common people, and many people purchased ukiyo-e to enjoy their works. Also, their works helped the common people find beauty in their daily lives.

The works of these painters became the prototype for modern manga and anime, playing a role in spreading Japanese art and culture to the world. Their works were valuable treasures that taught the importance of finding beauty in everyday life.

The works of Katsushika Hokusai and Utagawa Hiroshige are still loved by many people today. Their works are an essential part of conveying the splendor of Japanese art and culture.

Vocabulary

- 浮世絵 (Ukiyo-e) - Ukiyo-e

- 庶民 (Shomin) - Common people

- 葛飾北斎 (Katsushika Hokusai) - Katsushika Hokusai

- 歌川広重 (Utagawa Hiroshige) - Utagawa Hiroshige

- 美 (Bi) - Beauty

Comprehension Questions

浮世絵は何を描いたものでしたか？ What did ukiyo-e depict?

葛飾北斎と歌川広重はどのような作品を描きましたか？ What kind of works did Katsushika Hokusai and Utagawa Hiroshige create?

浮世絵はどのように庶民の生活を豊かにしましたか？ How did ukiyo-e enrich the lives of the common people?

ペリー提督と黒船の到来

むかしむかし、日本の江戸時代、幕府の力が全盛を極めていた時代がありました。その頃、幕府は強力な鎖国政策を推進し、外国との交流を制限していました。しかし、その静かな日々は、ある一人の外国人によって一変しました。

その名はマシュー・ペリー、アメリカ海軍の提督でした。彼は強大な「黒船」とともに、1854年に江戸湾に現れました。その船は黒く巨大で、日本の人々はその姿に驚き、恐怖を感じました。

ペリー提督は、日本を開国させ、自国との貿易を開始することを求めました。彼の要求は強硬で、日本の幕府は困惑しました。しかし、幕府はアメリカの圧力に屈し、開国という道を選びました。

この事件は、日本の歴史において重要な転換点となりました。外国との交流が増え、日本の文化や経済、政治が大きく変わり始めました。また、これは幕府の終焉と明治維新への道を開くきっかけともなりました。

しかし、その時点では誰もがその未来を予見することはできませんでした。彼らはただ、自分たちの生活が変わり始めることを感じ、新たな時代の幕開けを迎えました。

一方、ペリー提督は任務を完了し、アメリカへと帰国しました。彼は日本の開国を成し遂げた人物として、その名を歴史に刻みました。

この物語は、私たちが今日の世界を理解する上で重要な一部です。過去の出来事が現在の状況を形成し、未来へと繋がっていくことを示しています。

そして今、私たちはその歴史を見つめ、学び、考えることで、自分たちの未来をより良くすることができます。私たちは過去の経験から学び、それを未来へと繋げることができます。

だからこそ、私たちはこの物語を語り続け、次世代へと伝えていくのです。私たちは過去を忘れず、未来を創るために、学び続けるのです。

The Arrival of Commodore Perry and the Black Ships

Once upon a time, in the Edo period of Japan, there was a time when the shogunate was at its peak. At that time, the shogunate actively pursued a strong policy of isolationism, limiting exchanges with foreign countries. However, those quiet days were drastically changed by a foreigner.

His name was Matthew Perry, an admiral of the United States Navy. He appeared in Edo Bay in 1854 with his powerful "black ships". The ship was black and huge, and the people of Japan were surprised and terrified by its appearance.

Admiral Perry demanded that Japan open up and initiate trade with his country. His request was forceful, and the Japanese shogunate was bewildered. However, they yielded to American pressure and chose the path of opening the country.

This event was a significant turning point in Japanese history. The increase in exchanges with foreign countries began to dramatically change Japanese culture, economy, and politics. It also paved the way for the end of the shogunate and the Meiji Restoration.

However, at that point, no one could foresee that future. They just felt that their lives were beginning to change and welcomed the dawn of a new era.

On the other hand, Admiral Perry completed his mission and returned to America. He made his name in history as the person who opened Japan.

This story is an important part of understanding the world today. It shows how past events shape current situations and lead to the future.

And now, by looking at and learning from that history, and thinking, we can make our future better. We can learn from past experiences and connect them to the future.

That's why we keep telling this story and pass it on to the next generation. We continue to learn in order not to forget the past and to create the future.

Vocabulary

- 提督 (Teitoku) - Admiral

- 黒船 (Kurofune) - Black Ships

- 開国 (Kaikoku) - Opening of a country

- 幕府 (Bakufu) - Shogunate

- 明治維新 (Meiji Ishin) - Meiji Restoration

Comprehension Questions

ペリー提督が日本に何を求めましたか？ What did Admiral Perry demand from Japan?

ペリー提督の到来が日本にどのような影響を与えましたか？ How did the arrival of Admiral Perry affect Japan?

黒船とは何でしたか？ What were the Black Ships?

徳川時代の開国 – 日本が世界に開かれる

かつて、日本列島には、外の世界から隔てられた唯一の国がありました。その国名は日本、いわゆる「鎖国」の時代でした。しかし、ある日、一人の男が現れ、この閉ざされた国を世界に開くための一歩を踏み出しました。その男の名前は、徳川家康。

家康は、幼少期から戦の世界に身を置き、数々の困難を乗り越えてきました。彼の努力と知恵により、ついに全国の戦国大名を征服し、日本を統一したのです。その後、家康は新たな目標を定めました。それは、日本を世界に開くことでした。

しかし、この決断は国内外から様々な反発を呼びました。それでも家康は決意を固め、開国の準備を始めました。彼は、まず国内に情報を広め、国民の理解と協力を得ることから始めました。

その後、家康は西洋の商人との交渉を始めました。彼は彼らとの対話を通じて、日本と他国との友好関係を築き、文化交流を促進することを目指しました。そして、ついにその日が訪れました。日本が世界に開かれ、新たな時代が始まったのです。

家康の開国政策は、日本の経済と文化に大きな影響を与えました。外国との交流により、日本に新たな文化や技術が流入し、国民の生活は大きく変わりました。しかし、家康自身はその成果を見ることなく、老いてこの世を去りました。

その後も、家康の子孫たちは彼の志を継ぎ、日本を世界に開く道を進み続けました。それは、日本の未来を切り開くための道であり、多くの挑戦と困難に直面しながらも、彼らはその道を進み続けました。

そして、家康が開いた道は、日本が世界と共に歩むための道となりました。その道は、時には困難に満ちていましたが、日本人はそれを乗り越え、新たな時代を築いていきました。

これが、日本が世界に開かれるまでの物語でした。徳川家康の勇気と決断力、そして彼の子孫たちの努力により、日本は閉ざされた国から開国へと移行しました。そして、その歴史は今日まで続いています。

この物語は、我々が生きる現代社会にも大きな教訓を与えています。それは、困難を乗り越え、新たな道を切り開くための勇気と決断力、そして持続的な努力の重要性です。我々は、この教訓を胸に刻み、未来へと進むべきです。

The Opening of the Tokugawa Era - Japan Opens Up to the World

Once upon a time, there was an isolated country in the Japanese archipelago, separated from the outside world. The name of this country was Japan, during the so-called "closed country" period. However, one day, a man stepped forward to open this closed nation to the world. His name was Tokugawa Ieyasu.

From a young age, Ieyasu was immersed in the world of war, overcoming numerous difficulties. Through his efforts and wisdom, he finally conquered the feudal lords throughout the country and unified Japan. After that, Ieyasu set a new goal: to open Japan to the world.

However, this decision provoked various oppositions both domestically and abroad. Despite this, Ieyasu was determined and began preparations for opening the country. He started by spreading information within the country to gain understanding and cooperation from the people.

After that, Ieyasu began negotiations with Western merchants. Through dialogue with them, he aimed to establish friendly relationships between Japan and other countries and promote cultural exchange. Finally, the day arrived. Japan was opened to the world, and a new era began.

Ieyasu's policy of opening the country had a significant impact on Japan's economy and culture. The influx of new cultures and technologies into Japan through foreign exchanges dramatically changed the lives of the people. However, Ieyasu himself left this world in old age, without seeing the fruits of his labor.

Even after that, Ieyasu's descendants continued his will, continuing the path of opening Japan to the world. It was a path to forge the future of Japan, and despite facing many challenges and difficulties, they continued on this path.

The road that Ieyasu opened became the path for Japan to walk with the world. Although the road was often filled with difficulties, the Japanese people overcame them and built a new era.

This was the story of Japan's journey to opening up to the world. Through the courage and decision-making of Tokugawa Ieyasu and the efforts of his descendants, Japan transitioned from a closed country to an open one. And that history continues to this day.

This story provides a significant lesson to our modern society. It is the importance of courage and decision-making to overcome difficulties and open up new paths, and the importance of sustained effort. We should engrave this lesson in our hearts and move forward to the future.

Vocabulary

- 鎖国 (Sakoku) - Closed country

- 徳川家康 (Tokugawa Ieyasu) - Tokugawa Ieyasu

- 開国 (Kaikoku) - Opening of the country

- 西洋 (Seiyō) - The West

- 交渉 (Kōshō) - Negotiation

Comprehension Questions

徳川家康が日本を開国する決定を下した理由は何ですか？ What was the reason for Tokugawa Ieyasu's decision to open Japan to the world?

家康の開国政策は日本にどのような影響を与えましたか？ What impact did Ieyasu's policy of opening the country have on Japan?

家康の志を継いだのは誰で、彼らは何をしましたか？ Who inherited Ieyasu's will, and what did they do?

絹産業の発展

かつて、明治時代の日本に、小さな絹の工場がありました。その工場の主、鈴木一郎は、産業の未来を見つめ、絹産業を発展させることを決意していました。その頃、彼の工場はまだ小さなものでしたが、彼の情熱と努力のおかげで、徐々に絹の生産は増大しました。

ある日、一郎は洋の東西から来た商人たちに、自分の絹製品を売り込むことを決めました。彼は、最高品質の絹を作り出すために、一晩中働きました。そして、彼の努力は実り、その絹は海外の商人たちに大いに評価されました。

評価を受けた一郎の絹は、海外市場で非常に人気が出ました。これにより、彼の工場は急速に成長し、日本の絹産業は一夜にして躍進しました。その絹は、「日本の絹」として知られるようになりました。

しかし、一郎はまだ満足していませんでした。彼は、さらに品質を向上させ、日本の絹が世界中で最も価値あるものになるようにしました。彼は、新しい技術を探求し、絹の生産をより効率的にしました。

結果として、日本の絹産業は急速に発展しました。そして、一郎の工場はその中心となりました。その工場は、日本全国の絹生産者にとっての模範となりました。

一郎の努力により、日本の絹産業は世界の市場で主要な地位を占めるようになりました。そして、その成功は日本全体の繁栄につながりました。一郎の物語は、一人の男の情熱と努力が、国全体の産業をどのように発展させることができるかを示しています。

ほとんどの人々は、一郎の成功をただの偶然と思っていました。しかし、彼の成功は偶然ではなく、彼の情熱と努力の結果でした。彼の物語は、私たちに、どれだけの困難があっても、情熱と努力があれば、大きな成功を達成することができることを教えています。

一郎の物語は、明治時代の日本の絹産業の発展を象徴しています。彼の物語は、一人の男がどのようにして国全体の産業を発展させ、日本を絹の生産大国に変えたかを示しています。それは、一人の男の情熱と努力が、産業全体をどのように変えることができるかを示す、感動的な物語です。

Development of the Silk Industry

Once upon a time, in the Meiji era of Japan, there was a small silk factory. The owner of the factory, Ichiro Suzuki, was looking into the future of the industry and decided to develop the silk industry. At that time, his factory was still small, but thanks to his passion and efforts, the production of silk gradually increased.

One day, Ichiro decided to sell his silk products to merchants from the East and the West. He worked all night to produce the highest quality silk. And his efforts paid off, and his silk was highly valued by foreign merchants.

Ichiro's acclaimed silk became very popular in the overseas market. As a result, his factory grew rapidly, and the Japanese silk industry advanced overnight. The silk became known as "Japanese Silk."

However, Ichiro was not yet satisfied. He improved the quality even further and made Japanese silk the most valuable in the world. He explored new technologies and made silk production more efficient.

As a result, the Japanese silk industry developed rapidly. And Ichiro's factory became the center of it. The factory became a model for silk producers all over Japan.

Thanks to Ichiro's efforts, the Japanese silk industry came to occupy a major position in the world market. And his success led to prosperity throughout Japan. Ichiro's story shows how the passion and efforts of one man can develop an entire country's industry.

Most people thought of Ichiro's success as just a coincidence. However, his success was not a coincidence, but the result of his passion and effort. His story teaches us that, no matter how difficult it is, with passion and effort, we can achieve great success.

Ichiro's story symbolizes the development of the Japanese silk industry during the Meiji era. His story shows how one man developed an entire country's industry and turned Japan into a silk production powerhouse. It is a touching story that shows how the passion and effort of one man can change an entire industry.

Vocabulary

- 工場 (Kōjō) - Factory

- 商人 (Shōnin) - Merchant

- 絹 (Kinu) - Silk

- 品質 (Hinshitsu) - Quality

- 産業 (Sangyō) - Industry

Comprehension Questions

鈴木一郎はどのようにして絹産業を発展させましたか？ How did Ichiro Suzuki develop the silk industry?

一郎の絹はなぜ海外市場で人気が出ましたか？ Why did Ichiro's silk become popular in the overseas market?

一郎の成功は何によってもたらされましたか？ What brought about Ichiro's success?

明治時代と日露戦争の勇者たち

かつて、明治時代の日本に、西村という名の青年がいました。彼は庶民の出身でありながら、知識に飢え、学び続けることで自身の地位を向上させました。西村の知識は、彼が日本の近代化と文明開化の流れを理解するのに役立ちました。

1904 年、日露戦争が勃発しました。西村は日本の国土と国民を守るため、自ら戦地へと赴きました。彼は知識と勇気を武器に、仲間たちと共にロシア帝国と戦いました。

戦争は厳しく、多くの命が失われました。しかし、西村は常に前向きに、そして明晰に戦い続けました。彼の知識と戦略は、多くの戦闘で日本軍に勝利をもたらしました。

勝利の後、西村は日本に帰国しました。彼は英雄として迎えられ、その知識と経験を活かして日本の近代化に貢献しました。しかし、西村は常に謙虚であり、彼の成功は彼自身の努力だけでなく、日露戦争で命を捧げたすべての日本人の犠牲によるものだと語りました。

西村の物語は、日本の歴史の一部となり、勇気と知識の力を示す象徴となりました。彼の勇気と献身は、日本の国民の心に深く刻まれ、次世代へと受け継がれました。

The Heroes of the Meiji Era and the Russo-Japanese War

Once upon a time, during the Meiji era in Japan, there was a young man named Nishimura. Born of humble origins, he had a thirst for knowledge, which he used to elevate his status. Nishimura's knowledge helped him understand the flow of modernization and civilization in Japan.

In 1904, the Russo-Japanese War broke out. Nishimura, to protect Japan's lands and people, went to the battlefield himself. He fought against the Russian Empire with his knowledge and courage, along with his comrades.

The war was severe, and many lives were lost. However, Nishimura continued to fight positively and clearly. His knowledge and strategy brought victory to the Japanese military in many battles.

After the victory, Nishimura returned to Japan. He was welcomed as a hero and contributed to Japan's modernization using his knowledge and experience. However, Nishimura always remained humble, stating that his success was not only due to his efforts but also due to the sacrifices of all the Japanese who gave their lives in the Russo-Japanese War.

Nishimura's story became a part of Japan's history and a symbol of the power of courage and knowledge. His courage and dedication deeply imprinted in the hearts of the Japanese people and were passed on to the next generation.

Vocabulary

- 明治時代 (Meiji jidai) - Meiji era

- 日露戦争 (Nichi-Ro Sensō) - Russo-Japanese War

- 英雄 (Eiyū) - Hero

- 知識 (Chishiki) - Knowledge

- 勇気 (Yūki) - Courage

- 勝利 (Shōri) - Victory

- 献身 (Kenshin) - Dedication

Comprehension Questions

西村はどのようにして日露戦争に貢献しましたか？ How did Nishimura contribute to the Russo-Japanese War?

西村が帰国した後、彼はどのように日本の近代化に貢献しましたか？ How did Nishimura contribute to the modernization of Japan after he returned home?

西村は何によって英雄とされましたか？ What made Nishimura a hero?

昭和時代初期の革新者：田中健太郎

いにしえの昭和のころ、一人の男がいました。その男の名前は田中健太郎、彼は時代を超えた変革者でした。彼の家族は普通の農家で、簡素な生活を送っていましたが、健太郎は常に大きな夢を抱いていました。

ある日、彼は村の学校を卒業し、都市に行く決断をしました。その目的は、新しい知識を学び、故郷の人々の生活を豊かにすることでした。彼は電気という新しい発明に興味を持ち、それを勉強するために大学に入学しました。

数年後、彼は電気工学の学位を取得し、故郷に戻ってきました。人々は彼を温かく迎え、彼の新しい知識に期待を寄せました。健太郎は、村の電力供給を改善するためのプロジェクトを立ち上げ、電灯を各家庭に供給しました。

電灯が家々に供給されると、村人たちは驚きと喜びで溢れました。夜間でも作業ができ、子供たちは夜遅くまで勉強できるようになりました。田中健太郎の努力により、村の生活は大きく変わりました。

これがきっかけとなり、健太郎の名前は全国に広まりました。多くの村や町が彼を招き、電力供給の改善を求めました。彼は彼の知識と技術を共有し、日本全国の生活を豊かにするために尽力しました。

やがて、彼は大きな会社を設立し、全国に電力を供給するようになりました。彼はその成功を喜びましたが、常に謙虚さを忘れず、自分の原点を思い出しました。彼の努力と貢献により、昭和時代の初期は大きな進歩を遂げました。

健太郎が年を取るにつれ、彼の知識と経験は次の世代に引き継がれました。彼の遺産は今でも続いており、彼の影響は日本の電力供給と産業発展において重要な役割を果たしています。

Early Showa Era Innovator: Kenta Tanaka

In the ancient times of the Showa era, there was a man named Kenta Tanaka, an innovator beyond his time. His family were ordinary farmers living a simple life, but Kenta always harbored big dreams.

One day, he graduated from the village school and made the decision to go to the city. His purpose was to learn new knowledge and enrich the lives of the people in his hometown. He was interested in the new invention of electricity and enrolled in university to study it.

A few years later, he earned a degree in electrical engineering and returned to his hometown. People warmly welcomed him and looked forward to his new knowledge. Kenta launched a project to improve the village's power supply and provided electric lights to each household.

When the electric lights were supplied to the houses, the villagers were filled with surprise and joy. They could work even at night, and the children could study late into the night. Thanks to Kenta Tanaka's efforts, village life changed significantly.

This led to Kenta's name spreading nationwide. Many villages and towns invited him and asked for improvements in power supply. He shared his knowledge and skills and worked hard to enrich the lives of people all over Japan.

Eventually, he established a large company and started supplying electricity nationwide. He was pleased with his success, but always remembered his humility and remembered his roots. His efforts and contributions made significant progress in the early Showa era.

As Kenta got older, his knowledge and experience were passed on to the next generation. His legacy continues to this day, and his influence plays a significant role in Japan's power supply and industrial development.

Vocabulary

- 昭和 (Showa) - Showa era

- 革新者 (Kakushinsha) - Innovator

- 電気 (Denki) - Electricity

- 電力供給 (Denryoku kyokyu) - Power supply

- 会社 (Kaisha) - Company

- 遺産 (Isan) - Legacy

Comprehension Questions

田中健太郎は何を学びましたか？ What did Kenta Tanaka study?

彼は何を改善しましたか？ What did he improve?

なぜ彼の影響は重要でしたか？ Why was his influence important?

民主主義の芽生えとパーティーの興亡

昔々、戦国時代の終わりに、日本のある地方には、多くの小さな勢力が存在していました。それぞれ異なる思想と価値観を持ち、互いに競い合っていました。しかし、新たな風が吹き始め、一部の人々が民主主義の種を蒔き始めました。

ある日、かつては弱小だった一つの勢力が、民主主義の思想を掲げ、人々を巻き込んでいくことを決意しました。彼らは言論の自由、平等、公正を説き、多くの人々を惹きつけました。この勢力は次第に大きくなり、パーティーと呼ばれるようになりました。

このパーティーは、時には対立する他の勢力と協力し、時には争いながら、民主主義を広める活動を続けました。多くの人々がこの新しい思想に触れ、自由と平等を求める声が高まりました。

数年後、このパーティーは最も強大な勢力となり、地方の政治を担当することになりました。しかし、その後の数十年で、パーティーは徐々に力を失い、最終的には消滅しました。しかし、その遺産は残り、民主主義の思想は広く受け入れられるようになりました。

この物語は、ある地方での民主主義の芽生えとその発展、そしてパーティーの興亡を描いています。一見すると、パーティーの消滅は失敗のように見えるかもしれません。しかし、その過程で広がった民主主義の思想は、人々の生活を変え、社会を変革しました。

その地方の人々は、自由と平等を求める思想を持つようになり、それは次世代にも引き継がれました。そして、その思想は、地方から全国へと広がり、日本全体の政治や社会に影響を与えました。

そして今、私たちはその結果を見ています。民主主義の思想が広く受け入れられ、日本の社会や政治の基盤になっています。それは一つのパーティーの消滅から始まったのです。

この物語は、変化と挑戦、そして希望を象徴しています。それはまた、一つの思想がどのようにして社会を変え、人々の生活を改善する力を持つかを示しています。

The Dawn of Democracy and the Rise and Fall of Parties

Once upon a time, at the end of the Sengoku period, there were many small forces in a region of Japan. They each had different ideologies and values, and they competed with each other. However, a new wind began to blow, and some people started planting the seeds of democracy.

One day, a force that was once weak decided to advocate the idea of democracy and involve people. They preached freedom of speech, equality, and fairness, attracting many people. This force gradually grew and came to be called a party.

This party, sometimes collaborating with other conflicting forces and sometimes conflicting, continued activities to spread democracy. Many people touched this new idea, and the voice for freedom and equality grew louder.

Several years later, this party became the most powerful force and was in charge of local politics. However, over the next few decades, the party gradually lost its power and eventually disappeared. However, its legacy remained, and the idea of democracy became widely accepted.

This story depicts the germination and development of democracy in a region and the rise and fall of parties. At first glance, the disappearance of the party may seem like a failure. However, the spread of democratic ideas in the process has changed people's lives and transformed society.

The people of that region came to have the idea of seeking freedom and equality, which was passed on to the next generation. And that idea spread from the region to the whole country, affecting Japan's politics and society as a whole.

And now, we see the result. The idea of democracy is widely accepted and is the basis of Japan's social and political foundation. It all started with the disappearance of one party.

This story symbolizes change, challenge, and hope. It also shows how one idea can change society and improve people's lives.

Vocabulary

- 戦国時代 (Sengoku Jidai) - Sengoku period

- 民主主義 (Minshu-shugi) - Democracy

- 勢力 (Seiryoku) - Force

- パーティー (Pātī) - Party

- 消滅 (Shōmetsu) - Disappearance

Comprehension Questions

のようにして民主主義の思想が広まりましたか？ How did the idea of democracy spread?

パーティーはどのようにして力を失いましたか？ How did the party lose its power?

パーティーの消滅がどのように社会に影響を与えましたか？ How did the disappearance of the party affect society?

日本の降伏

かつて、昭和時代の日本に、名前を知られざる若者がいました。彼の名は剛で、彼は一人の漁師でした。しかし、彼の心の中には、常に国の未来を思い描く大志がありました。

1945 年、太平洋戦争の最終局面において、剛は海から帰還しました。彼の村は戦火により焼け野原と化しており、彼の家族も姿を消していました。剛は悲しみを押し残し、生き残るために必要な仕事に取り組みました。

ある日、日本の降伏が発表されました。剛は混乱の中、国と同胞の未来をどうすればよいのかを考えました。彼は村を再建し、生活を立て直すことを決意しました。

剛は村人たちと協力し、家を再建し、畑を耕し、漁を再開しました。彼はまた、子供たちに読み書きを教え、教育の重要性を説きました。村人たちは剛のリーダーシップを信頼し、彼を尊敬しました。

年月が経つにつれて、剛の村は再び生き生きとした活気を取り戻しました。剛はその成功を自身の力だけでなく、村人たちの協力と団結によるものと認識していました。

この物語は昭和時代の終焉とともに終わりますが、剛の努力と決意、そして村人たちの団結は、日本が困難を乗り越えて復興した象徴的な物語となります。

彼の物語は、一人の男の力と決意が、どのようにして大きな変化をもたらすことができるかを教えてくれます。それはまた、困難な時期においても、希望と団結がどれほど重要であるかを示しています。

Japan's Surrender

Once upon a time, in the Showa era of Japan, there was a young man whose name was not known. His name was Gou, and he was a fisherman. However, he always had a large ambition in his heart to envision the future of the country.

In 1945, at the final stage of the Pacific War, Gou returned from the sea. His village had been scorched by the war, and his family had disappeared. Gou suppressed his sadness and worked on the necessary tasks to survive.

One day, Japan's surrender was announced. Amid the confusion, Gou thought about what to do for the future of the country and his fellow countrymen. He decided to rebuild the village and rebuild his life.

Gou cooperated with the villagers to rebuild houses, cultivate fields, and resume fishing. He also taught children to read and write and preached the importance of education. The villagers trusted Gou's leadership and respected him.

As time passed, Gou's village regained its vibrant vitality. Gou recognized that this success was not only due to his own power but also due to the cooperation and unity of the villagers.

This story ends with the end of the Showa era, but Gou's efforts and determination, and the unity of the villagers, are a symbolic story of Japan overcoming difficulties and recovering.

His story teaches us how the power and determination of one man can bring about significant changes. It also shows how important hope and unity are in difficult times.

Vocabulary

- 昭和時代 (Showa Jidai) - Showa era

- 降伏 (Kōfuku) - Surrender

- 漁師 (Ryōshi) - Fisherman

- 再建 (Saiken) - Rebuilding

- 教育 (Kyōiku) - Education

Comprehension Questions

剛が何を決意したか？ What was the decision that Gou made?

剛が村の再建にどのように取り組んだか？ How did Gou work towards rebuilding the village?

この物語から何を学ぶことができますか？ What can you learn from this story?

漫画とアニメの台頭

昔々、1945年の夏、日本は二つの原子爆弾によって人類史上初めて戦争が終結しました。その後、日本は復興と国家再建の道を歩み始めました。その時代、一つの新しい芸術形式が生まれ、成長し始めました。それが、私たちが今日「漫画」と呼ぶものです。

初期の漫画家たちは、戦争の影響を受けた人々の心に希望をもたらすために、明るく楽しい物語を描くことを目指しました。その中でも、特に有名なのが手塚治虫で、彼の作品「鉄腕アトム」は、戦後の日本社会に大きな影響を与えました。

その後、漫画は急速に進化し、多様なジャンルが生まれました。少年、少女、青年、大人向けの漫画が登場し、それぞれの年齢層に合わせた物語が描かれるようになりました。その中でも、特に人気を博したのが、「ドラえもん」、「ワンピース」、「ナルト」などの作品です。

また、漫画の人気が高まるにつれて、その物語をアニメ化する動きも広がりました。アニメは、漫画の物語を視覚的に表現することで、より多くの視聴者に感動を与えることが可能となりました。その結果、アニメは日本のポップカルチャーの象徴となり、世界中にその影響力を広げました。

その後の時代、漫画とアニメは日本の文化の一部となり、世界に日本の文化を発信する重要なツールとなりました。今日では、これらのメディアは、日本の歴史、伝統、そして現代社会を理解するための窓となっています。

しかし、漫画とアニメが成長し続けるには、新たな才能が必要です。新しい世代の作家たちが、これらのメディアを通じて自分たちの物語を語り、新たな視点を提供することが期待されています。

The Rise of Manga and Anime

Once upon a time, in the summer of 1945, Japan became the first country in human history to end a war with two atomic bombs. After that, Japan began the journey of reconstruction and national rebuilding. During that period, a new form of art was born and began to grow. That is what we call "manga" today.

Early manga artists aimed to bring hope to the hearts of people affected by the war by creating bright and enjoyable stories. Among them, Osamu Tezuka was particularly famous, and his work "Astro Boy" had a significant impact on post-war Japanese society.

Subsequently, manga evolved rapidly, and various genres were born. Manga for boys, girls, youths, and adults appeared, and stories tailored to each age group began to be depicted. Among them, particularly popular works included "Doraemon," "One Piece," and "Naruto."

As the popularity of manga grew, there was also a movement to animate these stories. Anime made it possible to convey the stories of manga visually, touching more viewers. As a result, anime became a symbol of Japanese pop culture and spread its influence worldwide.

In the following era, manga and anime became part of Japanese culture and an important tool for transmitting Japanese culture to the world. Today, these media serve as windows for understanding Japan's history, traditions, and contemporary society.

However, for manga and anime to continue to grow, new talent is needed. The new generation of authors is expected to tell their stories through these media and provide new perspectives.

Vocabulary

- 戦後 (sengo) - Post-war

- 漫画 (manga) - Manga

- アニメ (anime) - Anime

- 手塚治虫 (Tezuka Osamu) - Osamu Tezuka

- 鉄腕アトム (Tetsuwan Atomu) - Astro Boy

- ドラえもん (Doraemon) - Doraemon

- ワンピース (Wan Pīsu) - One Piece

- ナルト (Naruto) - Naruto

Comprehension Questions

漫画はどのような時代背景の中で生まれましたか？ In what historical context was manga born?

手塚治虫の「鉄腕アトム」はどのような影響を与えましたか？ What impact did Osamu Tezuka's "Astro Boy" have?

漫画とアニメはどのように日本の文化を世界に発信していますか？ How do manga and anime transmit Japanese culture to the world?

日本食の普及：寿司の誕生

かつて、日本の地には、豊かな海が広がっていました。その海は、魚や海藻など、さまざまな海の幸を育んでいました。その中でも、特に寿司は日本の食文化の象徴となりました。

寿司の誕生は、保存食としての役割が大きかったと言われています。魚を塩と米で漬け込むことで、長期間保存することが可能となりました。これが寿司の原型であると考えられています。

しかし、寿司が現在の形に進化するまでには、長い時間がかかりました。まず、酢飯を用いるようになり、その上に新鮮な魚をのせる形式が生まれました。これが現在私たちが知る、握り寿司の始まりでした。

握り寿司は、人々にとって新鮮な魚を楽しむ手段となりました。また、手軽に食べられる食事として、町の人々に広まりました。特に、江戸時代になると握り寿司は大衆食として確固たる地位を築きました。

しかし、寿司が国外に広まるにはさらに時間がかかりました。戦後、日本の文化が世界に広く知られるようになり、寿司もまたその一部として認識されるようになりました。

今では、寿司は世界中で愛される日本食の代表格となりました。各地でさまざまなバリエーションが生まれ、それぞれの地域性を反映した寿司が楽しまれています。

寿司の魅力は、新鮮な魚の味を生かしながら、それぞれの具材が持つ個性を最大限に引き出すことにあります。また、一つ一つが手作りで、職人の技が光る点も特徴的です。

寿司の歴史は、日本の食文化の進化を物語っています。保存食から始まり、大衆食となり、そして世界へと広がっていった寿司の歴史は、日本の食文化がどのように発展してきたかを示しています。

これからも寿司は、その美味しさと多様性、そしてその背後にある日本の文化と歴史を伝える食事として、世界中の人々に愛され続けるでしょう。

The Spread of Japanese Cuisine: The Birth of Sushi

Once upon a time, in the land of Japan, there was a vast and fertile sea. This sea nurtured a variety of marine resources, including fish and seaweed. Among them, sushi in particular became a symbol of Japanese food culture.

The birth of sushi is said to have played a significant role as preserved food. By pickling fish in salt and rice, it became possible to preserve it for a long period. This is thought to be the prototype of sushi.

However, it took a long time for sushi to evolve into its current form. Firstly, sushi rice was used, and fresh fish was placed on top of it. This was the beginning of the nigiri sushi we know today.

Nigiri sushi became a way for people to enjoy fresh fish. Also, as a meal that could be easily eaten, it spread among the townspeople. Especially during the Edo period, nigiri sushi established a firm position as a popular food.

However, it took even more time for sushi to spread abroad. After World War II, Japanese culture became widely known worldwide, and sushi was also recognized as part of it.

Nowadays, sushi has become a representative of Japanese food loved all over the world. Various variations have been born in different places, and sushi reflecting each region's characteristics is enjoyed.

The charm of sushi lies in bringing out the maximum individuality of each ingredient while taking advantage of the taste of fresh fish. Also, each piece is handmade, and the craftsman's skill shines through.

The history of sushi tells the evolution of Japanese food culture. Starting as preserved food, becoming a popular meal, and then spreading to the world, the history of sushi shows how Japanese food culture has developed.

Sushi will continue to be loved by people around the world as a meal that conveys its deliciousness and diversity, as well as the culture and history behind it.

Vocabulary

- 寿司 (Sushi) - Sushi

- 保存食 (Hozonshoku) - Preserved food

- 酢飯 (Sushi-meshi) - Sushi rice

- 握り寿司 (Nigiri-zushi) - Nigiri sushi

- 大衆食 (Taishū-shoku) - Popular food

Comprehension Questions

寿司はどのようにして誕生しましたか？ How was sushi born?

握り寿司が日本で人気になった理由は何ですか？ What is the reason why nigiri sushi became popular in Japan?

寿司が世界に広まったきっかけは何ですか？ What led sushi to spread around the world?

コロナ禍に生き抜く勇者たち

それは 2020 年のこと、世界中が COVID-19 という病気に見舞われ、人々はその恐怖に震えていました。その中に、日本のある小さな町に住む一人の少年がいました。彼の名前はタロウと言い、彼はこの困難な時期を生き抜くために、日々奮闘していました。

COVID-19 の蔓延により、学校は閉鎖され、タロウは家で学習を続けなければなりませんでした。しかし、彼は勉強の傍ら、町の人々を助けるための方法を考えていました。彼は自身の小さな菜園で野菜を育て、それを町の人々に分け与えることにしました。

タロウの両親は彼の行動に感動し、自分たちもまた町の人々を助けるためにできることを探しました。母は手作りのマスクを作り始め、父は仕事を失った町の人々に仕事を提供するためのプロジェクトを立ち上げました。

タロウの家族の行動は、町の人々に大きな影響を与えました。彼らもまた、自分たちにできることを見つけては町の人々を助けるようになりました。町全体が一つになり、COVID-19 という困難に立ち向かう力を見つけました。

年月が経ち、2021 年になると、ワクチンが開発され、人々は少しずつ希望を見つけ始めました。タロウとその家族、そして町の人々は、この困難な時期を乗り越えることができました。彼らは困難を乗り越える力と、互いを助ける心を持つことの大切さを知りました。

この話は、私たちが困難な状況に直面したとき、互いに助け合い、共に力を合わせて戦うことの大切さを教えてくれます。タロウとその家族、そして町の人々は、COVID-19 という困難な時期を乗り越えるために、一つになり、互いの力を借りたのです。

The Heroes Who Survived the COVID Crisis

In the year 2020, when the world was hit by a disease called COVID-19, people trembled in fear. Among them, there was a boy living in a small town in Japan. His name was Taro, and he was striving every day to survive this difficult time.

With the spread of COVID-19, schools were closed, and Taro had to continue his studies at home. However, alongside his studies, he was thinking of ways to help the people in his town. He decided to grow vegetables in his small garden and share them with the people in his town.

Taro's parents were moved by his actions, and they too looked for ways to help the town's people. His mother started making handmade masks, and his father started a project to provide jobs for the people in the town who had lost their jobs.

The actions of Taro's family had a significant impact on the people in the town. They too started finding ways they could help and began assisting the townspeople. The entire town came together and found the strength to confront the adversity of COVID-19.

As time passed and it was 2021, vaccines were developed, and people slowly started to find hope. Taro, his family, and the townspeople were able to overcome this challenging period. They learned the importance of overcoming adversity and the importance of having a heart to help each other.

This story teaches us the importance of helping each other and fighting together when facing difficult situations. Taro, his family, and the townspeople came together and borrowed each other's strength to overcome the challenging times of COVID-19.

Vocabulary

- コロナ禍 (Koronaka) - COVID crisis

- 勇者 (Yūsha) - Hero

- 蔓延 (Man'en) - Spread

- マスク (Masuku) - Mask

- ワクチン (Wakuchin) - Vaccine

Comprehension Questions

タロウは何をして町の人々を助けましたか？What did Taro do to help the townspeople?

2021 年に何が起こりましたか？What happened in 2021?

この話から何を学びましたか？What did you learn from this story?

Conclusion

Learning the basics of any language is difficult, and the Japanese language can especially feel daunting for many newcomers. With that being said, if you were able to finish all of the lessons in this book, you have built a solid foundation in Japanese.

However, learning a language is a long process that rewards consistency. Even just listening and watching Japanese shows for 30 minutes a day can go a long way in improving your Japanese skills. We sincerely hope that you continue your Japanese language journey with the foundation you have built up and reach your goals, whether that be to understand the basics or speak like a native.

Thank you for choosing our book along your path to Japanese mastery and we hope that you obtained a lot of useful information! If you have any questions, comments, or even suggestions we would love to hear from you by email at Contact@worldwidenomadbooks.com. We greatly appreciate the feedback and this allows us to improve our books and provide the best language learning experience we can.

Thank you,

Worldwide Nomad Team